First World War
and Army of Occupation
War Diary
France, Belgium and Germany

20 DIVISION
Divisional Troops
84 Field Company Royal Engineers
23 July 1915 - 20 June 1919

WO95/2107/2

The Naval & Military Press Ltd
www.nmarchive.com
Published in association with The National Archives

Published by

The Naval & Military Press Ltd

Unit 10 Ridgewood Industrial Park,

Uckfield, East Sussex,

TN22 5QE England

Tel: +44 (0) 1825 749494

www.naval-military-press.com

www.nmarchive.com

This diary has been reprinted in facsimile from the original. Any imperfections are inevitably reproduced and the quality may fall short of modern type and cartographic standards.

© Crown Copyright
Images reproduced by permission of The National Archives, London, England, 2015.

Contents

Document type	Place/Title	Date From	Date To
Miscellaneous	2107/3		
Heading	20th Division Divl Engineers C.R.E. 84th Field Coy. R.E. Jly 1915-June 1919		
Heading	84th F.C.R.E. Vol I Jly To Aug 15		
War Diary	Havre	23/07/1915	23/07/1915
War Diary	Wizernes	24/07/1915	24/07/1915
War Diary	Hallines	25/07/1915	25/07/1915
War Diary	Au Souverain Near Hazebrouck	28/07/1915	28/07/1915
Heading	No Ate Boom Near Merris	29/07/1915	29/07/1915
War Diary	La Becque West of Steenwerck	30/07/1915	30/07/1915
War Diary	La Becque	02/08/1915	04/08/1915
War Diary	Erquinghem	03/08/1915	16/08/1915
War Diary	Outtersteene	17/08/1915	27/08/1915
War Diary	Rue De La Lys	28/08/1915	31/08/1915
Heading	84th F.C.R.E. Vol II Sept 1-15		
War Diary	Rue De La Lys	01/09/1915	04/09/1915
War Diary	Rue de Bliache	05/09/1915	28/09/1915
War Diary	Lanentie	30/09/1915	01/10/1915
War Diary	Lanentie	05/09/1915	30/09/1915
Heading	84th F.C.R.E. Vol 3 Oct 15		
War Diary	Laventie	01/10/1915	31/10/1915
Heading	84th F.C.R.E. Vol 4 Nov 15		
War Diary	Laventie	01/11/1915	30/11/1915
War Diary	Bac St Maur	20/11/1915	20/11/1915
Heading	84th F.C.R.E. Vol 5		
War Diary	Bac St Maur	02/12/1915	23/12/1915
Heading	84th F.C.R.E. Vol 6 Jan 16		
War Diary	Bac St Maur	01/01/1916	09/01/1916
War Diary	Nouveau Monde	09/01/1916	22/01/1916
War Diary	Arneke	23/01/1916	31/01/1916
Heading	84th F.C.R.E. Vol 7		
War Diary	Arneke	01/03/1916	03/03/1916
War Diary	Ledringham	04/03/1916	12/03/1916
War Diary	Watou	12/03/1916	13/03/1916
War Diary	Camp. 2 Miles S W of Elverdinghe Sheet 27 A 24 G 7 3	13/03/1916	29/03/1916
Heading	84 F.C.R.E. Vol 8		
War Diary	Camp. 2 Miles S W of Elverdinghe Sheet 28 A24 b.7.3	01/03/1916	31/03/1916
War Diary	Camp. 2 Miles S W of Elverdinghe Sheet 28 A24 b.7.3	01/04/1916	30/04/1916
Miscellaneous	D A G 3rd Echelon	01/07/1916	01/07/1916
War Diary	Herzeele	01/05/1916	16/05/1916
War Diary	Ypres	17/05/1916	30/06/1916
Heading	84th Field Company R.E. July 1916		
War Diary	Ypres	01/07/1916	15/07/1916
War Diary	La Clytte	15/07/1916	25/07/1916
War Diary	Halloy	25/07/1916	31/07/1916
Heading	20th Divisional Engineers. 84th Field Company R.E. August 1916		
War Diary	Courcelles	01/08/1916	07/08/1916
War Diary	Rossignol FM.	08/08/1916	27/08/1916

War Diary	F12 c.6.9 Sheet 62 D	27/08/1916	31/08/1916
Heading	20th Divisional Engineers. 84th Field Company R.E. September 1916		
War Diary	F12.c.6.9 Sheet 62D	01/09/1916	06/09/1916
War Diary	Sand Pits To Mericourt	08/09/1916	16/09/1916
War Diary	Waterlot Fm	17/09/1916	19/09/1916
War Diary	Burnafay Wood	17/09/1916	19/09/1916
War Diary	Meaulte	22/09/1916	22/09/1916
War Diary	Citadel	25/09/1916	25/09/1916
War Diary	Maltzhorn Valley	26/09/1916	27/09/1916
War Diary	Carnoy	27/09/1916	28/09/1916
War Diary	Longueval	29/09/1916	29/09/1916
Heading	20th Divisional Engineers. 84th Field Company R.E. October 1916		
Heading	84th Field Coy Vol 15		
War Diary	Longueval	01/10/1916	07/10/1916
War Diary	Maricourt	08/10/1916	09/10/1916
War Diary	Meaulte	10/10/1916	15/10/1916
War Diary	Citadel	18/10/1916	18/10/1916
War Diary	A 2 d 5 0 Albert Sheet	19/10/1916	25/10/1916
War Diary	Conde	26/10/1916	31/10/1916
Heading	20th Divisional Engineers. 84th Field Company R.E. November 1916		
War Diary	Bertangles	08/11/1916	08/11/1916
War Diary	Allonville	08/11/1916	08/11/1916
War Diary	Picquigny	08/11/1916	13/11/1916
War Diary	Laleu	14/11/1916	19/11/1916
War Diary	Daours	19/11/1916	27/11/1916
War Diary	Citadel	27/11/1916	27/11/1916
War Diary	Mansel Camp	28/11/1916	30/11/1916
Heading	20th Divisional Engineers 84th Field Company R.E. December 1916		
War Diary	Mansel Camp	01/12/1916	31/12/1916
Heading	War Diary of The 84th Field Company R.E. January 1917 Vol 18		
War Diary	Meaulte	01/01/1917	15/01/1917
War Diary	Combles	20/01/1917	20/01/1917
War Diary	Combles	18/01/1917	26/01/1917
War Diary	Grove Town	31/01/1917	06/02/1917
War Diary	Bernafay Wood S.29.c	07/02/1917	01/03/1917
War Diary	S 29 C	12/03/1917	15/03/1917
War Diary	Bovril	16/03/1917	16/03/1917
War Diary	Transloy	19/03/1917	29/03/1917
War Diary	Le Transloy	30/03/1917	30/03/1917
War Diary	Ytres	01/04/1917	01/04/1917
War Diary	Royaulcourt	01/05/1917	19/05/1917
War Diary	Ytres	20/05/1917	31/05/1917
War Diary	Lagnicourt Beugny Road	01/06/1917	01/06/1917
War Diary	Favreuil	01/06/1917	22/06/1917
War Diary	Noreuil	23/06/1917	28/06/1917
War Diary	Bihucourt	28/06/1917	30/06/1917
War Diary	Bihucourt (Lens II)	01/07/1917	01/07/1917
War Diary	Bernaville	18/03/1917	18/03/1917
War Diary	Bernaville	03/07/1917	13/07/1917
War Diary	Haandekot	21/07/1917	22/07/1917
War Diary	Haandekot E.4.c.8.1 Sheet 27	27/07/1917	30/07/1917

War Diary	Haandekot E.4.c.8.1 Sheet 27		15/07/1917	15/07/1917
War Diary	Haandekot E.4.c.8.1 Sheet 27		01/08/1917	06/08/1917
War Diary	Canal Bank C.19.c.2.6		07/08/1917	18/08/1917
War Diary	P 5 area (Proven)		19/08/1917	31/08/1917
War Diary	Welsh Fm Elverdinghe		01/09/1917	20/09/1917
War Diary	Canal Bank C.19.a.0.7 Sheet 28		21/09/1917	30/09/1917
War Diary	Proven Sheet 27		01/10/1917	01/10/1917
War Diary	Bapaume Sheet 57 C		02/10/1917	03/10/1917
War Diary	Ytres Sheet 57 C		03/10/1917	07/10/1917
War Diary	Sorel (Sheet 57c)		08/10/1917	08/10/1917
War Diary	Heudecourt		09/10/1917	31/10/1917
War Diary	Heudecourt Sheet 57 C		31/10/1917	30/11/1917
War Diary			27/11/1917	29/11/1917
War Diary			20/11/1917	01/12/1917
War Diary	Nurlu		03/12/1917	30/12/1917
War Diary	Nurlu		17/12/1917	17/12/1917
War Diary	Dugouts S of Marcoing L 34 b 1.3		30/12/1917	30/12/1917
War Diary	Nurlu		03/12/1917	03/12/1917
War Diary	Villers-Pluich		30/10/1917	03/12/1917
War Diary	Nurlu		03/12/1917	03/12/1917
War Diary	Nurlu		03/12/1917	18/01/1918
War Diary	Scottish Wood H 35 b. Sheet 28 NW		19/01/1918	30/01/1918
War Diary	H Q At Scottish Wd H 35 b Sheet 28 NW		31/01/1918	31/01/1918
War Diary	Scottish Wood H 35 b Sheet 28 NW		01/02/1918	20/02/1918
War Diary	Heuringhem (Sheet Hazebrouck 5a)		21/02/1918	28/02/1918
War Diary	Tirlancourt (Sheet 66D)		28/02/1918	28/02/1918
Heading	20th Divisional Engineers 84th Field Company R.E. March 1918			
War Diary	Tirlancourt (Sheet 66D)		01/03/1918	03/03/1918
War Diary	Canizy		04/03/1918	21/03/1918
War Diary	Ham		21/03/1918	23/03/1918
War Diary	Oleezy		23/03/1918	31/03/1918
War Diary	Ham		21/03/1918	27/03/1918
War Diary			01/04/1918	12/04/1918
War Diary	Oust Marest		12/04/1918	18/04/1918
War Diary	Marquay		19/04/1918	30/04/1918
War Diary	Camblain-L'Abbe		30/04/1918	02/05/1918
War Diary	Ablain St Nazaire		02/05/1918	31/05/1918
War Diary	Ablain St Nazaire		19/05/1918	28/05/1918
War Diary	Ablain St Nazaire		23/05/1918	23/05/1918
War Diary	Ablain St Nazaire		19/05/1918	19/05/1918
War Diary	Ablain St Nazaire (Lens II)		01/06/1918	31/07/1918
War Diary	Ablain St Nazaire		01/08/1918	30/08/1918
War Diary	La Targette		31/08/1918	31/08/1918
War Diary	La Targette (Lens II)		01/09/1918	30/09/1918
War Diary	La Targette		30/09/1918	30/09/1918
War Diary	La Targette (Sheet Lens II)		01/10/1918	04/10/1918
War Diary	Thelus (Sheet Lens II)		05/10/1918	31/10/1918
War Diary	Bethencourt		31/10/1918	31/10/1918
War Diary	Bapaume		01/11/1918	01/11/1918
War Diary	Cambrai		02/11/1918	02/11/1918
War Diary	Cagnoncles		03/11/1918	03/11/1918
War Diary	St Aubert		04/11/1918	05/11/1918
War Diary	Vendegies		06/11/1918	06/11/1918
War Diary	Sepmeries		07/11/1918	07/11/1918
War Diary	Sepmeries K 36 d		08/11/1918	08/11/1918

War Diary	Wargnies-Le-Petit G 34 a	09/11/1918	10/11/1918
War Diary	Fiegnies J.22.b	10/11/1918	11/11/1918
War Diary	Bois Brule K.27.b	12/11/1918	22/11/1918
War Diary	Feignies J.29.c.8.3	23/11/1918	23/11/1918
War Diary	La Flamengrie H.13.a.9.2	24/11/1918	24/11/1918
War Diary	Wargnies-Le-Petit G.28.a.5.1	25/11/1918	25/11/1918
War Diary	Vendegies Q.7.d.2.2	26/11/1918	27/11/1918
War Diary	Cargnoncles Valenciennes 1/10,000 D4	28/11/1918	30/11/1918
War Diary	Cargnoncles	30/11/1918	30/11/1918
War Diary	Cambrai	01/12/1918	02/12/1918
War Diary	Famechon Map-1/10,000 Lens (F 5)	03/12/1918	06/12/1918
War Diary	Famechon	07/12/1918	27/12/1918
War Diary	Famechon B.26.d.3.6	28/12/1918	31/01/1919
War Diary	Famechon C.26.d	01/02/1919	20/06/1919

2107/3

20TH DIVISION
DIVL ENGINEERS

C. R. E.
84TH FIELD COY. R.E.
JLY 1915 – JUNE 1919

20th Division

121/6787

84th F.C.R.E.
Vol: I

Jly & Aug 15

June '19

✓

84th Field Coy R.E
20th Division

WAR DIARY or INTELLIGENCE SUMMARY.
(Erase heading not required.)

Army Form C. 2118.

Place	Date	Hour	Summary of Events and Information	Remarks and references to Appendices
HAVRE	23/7/15	7.30 a.m.	Company disembarked	
		12.15 a.m.	Arrived Rest Camp No 5.	
	24/7/15	2.59 a.m.	Left GARE MARITIME	
WIZERNES		10.30 p.m.	Arrived WIZERNES	
HALLINES	25/7/15	1 a.m.	" " in Billets at HALLINES – Concentration Area – billetted in 61st Brigade Area.	
AU SOUVERAIN near HAZEBROUCK	28/7/15	2.40 p.m.	Marched from HALLINES to AU SOUVERAIN & bivouaced there	
NOATE BOOM near MERRIS	29/7/15	12-0 nn	" " AU SOUVERAIN to NOATE BOOM "	
LA BECQUE (West of STEENWERCK)	30/7/15	11.30 a.m.	Changed from NOATE BOOM to LA BECQUE as the company had been put into the former place by the billetting party in error	
LA BECQUE	2/8/15		Part of H.Q. with Nos 1 & 2 Sections went to the 17th Coy at ERQUINGHEM LYS for instruction at the trenches. Nos 3 & 4 Sections employed on well construction at LA BECQUE & LE MORTIER S. of STEENWERCK	
" "	3/8/15		Nos 2 & 3 Sections making wells at LA BECQUE & LE MORTIER.	
" "	4/8/15			
ERQUINGHEM	3/8/15		Nos 1 & 4 Sections working with 17th Coy R.E. in 80th Brigade Section of trenches near RUE du BOIS. No 1 on a breast work in support line. No 4 making wired revetment for back of a communication trench – (Bright Walk) rear of No 59 trench.	
" "	4/8/15		No 1 Section continued on work of 3/8. 4 sappers were taken 4 at a time to the fire trenches.	
" "	5/8/15		No 1 Section – strengthening trenches in support line. No 4 Section – improving a breastwork by sandbag revetments & traverses. H.Q. & Nos 2 & 3 Sections arrived at ERQUINGHEM at 4.0 p.m.	
" "	6/8/15		No 2 Section – strengthening trenches. No 4 Section work as on 5/8. O.C. visited trenches with O.C. 17th Coy. No 1 Section – (Night work) Breastwork communication near COWGATE AVENUE	
" "	7/8/15		No 2 Section improving breastwork (started by No 4). No 3 Section strengthening trenches. O.C. visited trenches with G.O.C. 27th Div. & Brigadier 80th Bde. No 1 Section (Night work) Breastwork communication near COWGATE AVENUE	

WAR DIARY or INTELLIGENCE SUMMARY.

(Erase heading not required.)

Army Form C. 2118

Instructions regarding War Diaries and Intelligence Summaries are contained in F. S. Regs., Part II. and the Staff Manual respectively. Title pages will be prepared in manuscript.

Place	Date	Hour	Summary of Events and Information	Remarks and references to Appendices
ERQUINGHEM	9.8.15	6.30am	Nos 1 & 4 Sections proceeded to LA BECQUE. No 2 Section - improving breast work. No 3 " " - making communication trench	
	10.8.15		No 2 Section - communication trench - Rue du Bois. No 3 " " - improving breast work & constructing emplacement for machine gun No 62 front trench	
	11.8.15		as on 10th	
	12.8.15		No 2 Section completing revetting of fire trenches - rear of No 59 front trenches. No 3 " " - making dug outs near RAILWAY AVENUE.	
	13.8.15		Nos 2 & 3 Sections - communication trenches & dug outs near RAILWAY AVENUE.	
	14.8.15		Same as 13.8.15.	
	16.8.15		Nos 2 & 3 Sections pontooning.	
	10 to 16/8/15		Nos 1 & 4 Sections - making wells & 30 yds Rifle Ranges - in neighbourhood of MERRIS	
			& STEENJE	
OUTTERSTEENE	17/8/15		Nos 2 & 3 Sects joined Nos 1 & 4 at OUTTERSTEENE near MERRIS	
	17 to 21 /8/15		Four sections constructing wells & Rifle Ranges	
	/8/15			
	22/8/15		No 4 Sect. proceeded to ERQUINGHEM to work on trenches with 1st Wessex Field Coy R.E.	
	22) 23)8/15 24)		Nos 1, 2 & 3 continue work on Wells & Rifle Ranges	
	25/8/15		No 2 Sect. proceeded to ESTAIRES for work in connection with altering Starch Factory to convert it for Baths & Laundry for 20th Division	
	25) 26) 8/15		No 1 & No 3 - Wells & Ranges OUTTERSTEENE. No 2 - Baths & Laundry ESTAIRES. No 4 - Trenches ERQUINGHEM.	
	27/8/15		No 1 & No 3 proceeded to billets at RUE de la LYS near SAILLY for work on posts in CROIX BARBEE-FLEURBAIX System behind front line of System taken over by the 20th Div. No 2 & No 4 work as on 26/8	

WAR DIARY

84th Field Coy R.E. - 20th Division.

Army Form C. 2118.

Place	Date	Hour	Summary of Events and Information	Remarks and references to Appendices
Rue de la Lys	28/8/15		Taking over work on the allotted system. No 4 Sect. rejoins H.Q. & No 1 & 3 Sections. No 2 Sect. continues work at factory ESTAIRES.	
"	29/8/15 to 31/8/15		No 1 & 3 Sections improving & constructing Posts. No 2 Section continue work at factory. No 4 Section - Bridges for emergency roads. Pontoon bridges & barges for making lifting bridge fit for wheel traffic - all on R. LYS - East of ESTAIRES in 20th Div area.	

H.C. Christie
Major R.E.
O.C. 84th Fd Coy R.E.
1/9/15

20th Division

121/6971

84th F.C.R.E.

vol II

Sept. 15

✓

84th Field Cy RE

WAR DIARY
or
~~INTELLIGENCE SUMMARY~~
(Erase heading not required.)

Army Form C. 2118.

84th FCRE

Place	Date	Hour	Summary of Events and Information	Remarks and references to Appendices
RUE de la LYS	1.9.15 to 4.9.15		Nos 1 & 3 Sections constructing & improving posts. No 2 Section at work on Laundry & Baths ESTAIRES. No 4 Section continuing making approaches for pontoon bridges & lifting bridge near NOUVEAU MONDE on River LYS	
RUE de BLIACHE	5.9.15		Nos 1 & 4 Sections proceeded with 61st Brigade - who take over part of line from 8th Divn. from about N 4 d to about N 3 c. Remainder of Coy remained at RUE de la LYS to work pontoon bridges, complete laundry, make emergency roads & prepare material for Nos 1 & 4 Sections. Work of Nos 1 & 4 Section comprised thickening parapets & putting dug outs in them improving communication trenches by deepening & widening.	
	9.9.15		Lieut Currie joined in place of Lieut Marsin - to be Adjutant	
	11.9.15		" Watson " " " " Romer sick	
	11.9.15		Bath & Laundry at ESTAIRES opened.	
	12.9.15		Lieut Train & most of No 3 Section joined 1 & 4 Sections at RUE di BLIA CAE BALLET	
	13.9.15		Mine exploded in front of parapet about Sect 2 R. New parapet started in rear. Old parapet on 14.9.15	
	16/17.9.15		Lieut Currie started to lay wire in front of new parapet mentioned above he assisted in rallying men, who were in a panic when trench mortars fell among them.	

84th Field Coy R.E.

WAR DIARY ~~or INTELLIGENCE SUMMARY~~

Army Form C. 2118.

(Erase heading not required.)

Place	Date	Hour	Summary of Events and Information	Remarks and references to Appendices
Rue de Bliache	15.9.15 to 24.9.15		Nos 1, 3 & 4 Sections assisting infantry to make dug outs & bomb proof shelters as a protection against bombardment.	
	21.9.15 to 24.9.15		Bombardment of German trenches. Sections employed as above assisted by 2 companies of 11th Durham Light Infantry - Pioneers.	
	24.9.15		Nos 1, 3, & 4 Sections proceeded to trenches in evening & went into dug outs in support line 2P, with a view to taking part in any advance made against German lines, & to make a communication from our line to German if a lodgement effected by 6th R.B.	
	25.9.15		3 & 4 Sections at night repaired parapet in 2S damaged by H.E. shell during the day, a difficult matter under fire & in very wet ground.	
	26.9.15		Repairing parapets.	
	27.9.15		1, 3 & 4 Sects returned to billet at Rue de Bliache 3.0 am	
	28.9.15		Moved billet (1, 3 & 4 Sects) to Rue de la Lys. 61st Bde changed line & limits now are N.10 c 3/6 to N.14 a. 0/5.	
Laventie	30.9.15 & 1.10.15		The Company moved into billets at Laventie	
	5.9.15 to 30.9.15		No 2 Section & part of No 3 (all transport) with the Infantry. Carpenters were at Billet Rue de la Lys. completing laundry & baths, improving roads, looking after bridges, looking after Infantry parties at Le Drumez & La Flinque Posts	

30th Division

121/7595

84th F.C.R.E.
Vol 3

Oct 15

34th Field Coy RE

WAR DIARY
or
INTELLIGENCE SUMMARY
(Erase heading not required.)

Army Form C. 2118

Instructions regarding War Diaries and Intelligence Summaries are contained in F. S. Regs., Part II. and the Staff Manual respectively. Title pages will be prepared in manuscript.

Place	Date	Hour	Summary of Events and Information	Remarks and references to Appendices
LAVENTIE	1.10.15		No 2 Section joined the rest of the company. All transport ditto.	Company still attached to 6pt Brigade Ed "trench" for work in their brigade billets area
	1.10.15 to 10.10.15		No 1 Section laying trench boards in Avenues, improving front-line parapets dug outs & paradoses.	
			No 2 Section - improving horse watering arrangements RIVER LYS - sundry work at Baths & Laundry preparing yard at billet for workshops &c.	
			No 3 Section } same work as No 1 & also clearing ditches near the front-line for drainage purposes	
			No 4 Section	
	11.10.15 to 17.10.15		No 1 Section. horse watering arrangements. preparing oil engine & circular saw in LAVENTIE for work - sundry work in Company Yard.	
			No 2 & 3 Sections continuing trench boards, drainage, & improvement of front line	
			No 4 Section - commenced erecting huts for winter accommodation & repairing billets in Brigade area for ditto.	
	18.10.15 to 24.10.15		No 1 & 2 Sections - trench boards in front line, & avenues & improvement of ditches for drainage - also constructing dug outs & improving parapet front line.	
			No 3 Section - sundry work near billets - troughs, pumps for watering horses &c.	
			No 4 Section - Hutting & billet repairs.	
	25.10.15 to 31.10.15		Similar work to the above except that about 20 men were working for 96th Coy RE, putting in recesses for gas cylinders in 59th Bde line 13 recesses also put in 61st Bde line	

30th Division

84th F.C.R.E.
vol: 4

121/7678

Nov. 15

84th Field Coy R.E.

WAR DIARY
INTELLIGENCE SUMMARY.

Place	Date	Hour	Summary of Events and Information	Remarks and references to Appendices
LAVENTIE	1.11.15 to 7.11.15		Nos 1 & 2 Section - Work in the Front Line & Communication Trenches - Clearing ditches for drainage - laying trench boards in front line - making improvements to parapets paradoes & dug outs - constructing Machine gun emplacements. No 3 Sect. Incidental repairs to billets, breastworks & posts. No 4 Sect - Hutting. Man from each section & 30 Infantry preparing materials in Company yard.	
	8.11.15 to 14.11.15		Work as above.	
	15.11.15 to 21.11.15		Work as above, but No 3 Sect takes the place of No 1. Leaving Nos 2 & 3 in trenches 1 & 4 out.	
	22.11.15 to 30.11.15		" " " No 4 Sect takes the place of No 2 " No 3 & 4 Sects in trenches 1 & 2 out.	
BAC ST MAUR	20.11.15		The Company moved to billets at BAC ST MAUR as the 61st Brigade shifted its line to the left, taking up on the 24th from BOND St exclusive to N/10/C 9/2. 59th Brigade on right till 20.11.15 then the Guards Division. 23d " " left " 20.11.15 " the 60th Brigade.	

84th FCRE.
vol. 5

181

7910

84th Field Coy RE

WAR DIARY or INTELLIGENCE SUMMARY.

Army Form C. 2118.

(Erase heading not required.)

Place	Date	Hour	Summary of Events and Information	Remarks and references to Appendices
BAC ST MAUR	2/12/15		Lieut Norman wounded.	
	4/12/15		The Company went into reserve & was employed until 14.12.15 on cutting horse shelters & repairs to billets.	
	6/12/15		Lieut Winby joined.	
	14/12/15		Took over new line N4d 7/2 to N6a 8/0. Work on communication trenches, repairs to parapets. WELL FARM Salient closed, repairs & extensions. One section working on huts.	
	18/12/15		Lieut Currie wounded, died on 19th.	
	23/12/15		Lieut White joined.	

31.12.15

HP Christie
Major RE OC 84th Coy RE

S.L. & J.C.R.L.

vol. 6
Jan '16

84th Field Coy R.E

WAR DIARY
or
INTELLIGENCE SUMMARY.

(Erase heading not required.)

Army Form C. 2118.

Place	Date	Hour	Summary of Events and Information	Remarks and references to Appendices
BAC ST MAUR	1.1.16 to 9.1.16		Two & a half sections employed in the trenches Map 36 - N4d 7/2 to N6a 3/0. Work on Communication Trenches. WELL FM Salient Clearance & repairs to front line parapet.	
NOUVEAU MONDE	9.1.16		Division goes into Reserve in STEENBECQUE AREA. The company goes to Billets at NOUVEAU MONDE for work under C.E 3rd Corps on FLEURBAIX & LAVENTIE North Posts.	
	21.1.16		The Division ordered to join the 2nd Army. Company marches to STEENBECQUE.	
	22.1.16		Company marches to near ARNEKE.	
ARNEKE	23.1.16 -27.1.16		Sectional Training & Rest continued.	
	27.1.16		Major H.S. Christie promoted to Temp: Lt Colonel & proceeds as C.R.E. 6th Divn. handing over the command of the Company to Captain P.G. Huddleston R.E. Lt Norman rejoined.	
	30/1/16		Lt Manisty transferred to this company in place of 2nd Lt Watson transferred to the 83rd Field Co R.E	
	31/1/16		Company still in training & rest.	

P.G. Huddleston
Capt R.E
O.C 84th Field Co R.E

3/2/16

Feb 1st 1916

84 ē T. E. R. E.
Vol: 7

20
THIS IS A
FEBRUARY DIARY
FALSELY DATED THROUGHOUT

FEBRUARY

84th Fd Co R.E.

WAR DIARY

Army Form C. 2118.

Place	Date	Hour	Summary of Events and Information	Remarks and references to Appendices
ARNEKE	1-3-16 to 3-3-16		Training and rest and Company moved to LEDRINGHAM	
LEDRINGHAM	4-3-16 to 12-3-16		Training & rest continued and moved to take over from 14th Division RE in line N of Ypres from BOESINGHE to BRIELEN. LIEUT WINBY evacuated to No 20 Stationary Hospital on 9th	
WATOU	12-3-16 to 13-3-16		ditto	
CAMP 2 MILES SW of ELVERDINGHE SHEET 27 A 24, 6 7.3	13-3-16		Moved to new camp and same night 2 Sections moved to take over maintainance of bridges, 7Z to 4 inclusive on extreme left of British and right of French line.	
DITTO	14-3-16 to 21-3-16		84th in Reserve. No 3 & 4 - ½ Sections remained in Dugouts on Canal Bank, other ½ Sections went up nightly for work there & on bridges. No 1 & 2 Sections employed on hutting & miscellaneous duties in Divisional Reserve	
	22-3-16 to 27-3-16		No 1 & 2 Sections replaced No 3 & 4 Sections in maintenance of Bridges.	
	27-3-16 to 28-3-16	night	Took over Front Line left Section, East of the Canal Bank, from Bridge 7Z on French Right to line from Junction D22-D21 to Bridge 6. Affiliated to 61st Brigade. 2/Lt EARL joined vice Lt. WINBY	
	29-3-16		Still O.C. & 2 Sections in Dugouts, 2 Sections in rear in Billets	

B.G. [illegible] Lt RE
for P.G. Huddleston Capt RE
March 31/16   O.C. 84th Field Co RE

$$8\sqrt{847622}$$

WAR DIARY *or* **INTELLIGENCE SUMMARY**

814th Field Co. R.E.

Army Form C. 2118.

Place	Date	Hour	Summary of Events and Information	Remarks and references to Appendices
CAMP 2 MILES SW OF ELVERDINGHE SHEET 28 A24 b 7.3	1/3/16	—	No 1 & 2 Sections in dugouts in Canal Bank. Working on front line trenches, affiliated to left Brigade. Nos 3 & 4 Sections in reserve making up revetting material for front line. 2/Lt Martin 7th Som L.I. attached, took charge of organisation for delivering material on to site of work.	
	2nd/3rd	—	Nos 3 & 4 Sections relieved Nos 1 & 2 Sections.	
	10/3/16	—	Nos 1 & 2 Sections relieved Nos 3 & 4 Sections. Lt Wemby resumed for duty. Temporarily attached to 96th Field Co R.E.	
	18/3/16	—	Nos 3 & 4 Sections relieved Nos 1 & 2 Sections.	
	19/20			
	25/3/16		Captain Huddleston R.E. O.C. Killed in Action. Company temporarily commanded by Lieut P.S. Norman R.E. (T.C.) Capt. Huddleston's remains buried at OLIVERS FARM Cemetery B 13 b 1.5. Sheet 28.	
	26/3/16		Nos 1 & 2 Sections relieved Nos 3 & 4 Sections	
	28/3/16 } 29/3/16 }		2/Lt Hill temporarily attached for duty from 83rd Field Co R.E.	
	28/3/16		Lt Ward acting Adjutant.	
	28/3/16		Captain M.A.H. Scott R.E. took over command of the Company.	
	30/3/16		Lt White transferred to 83rd Field Co R.E.	
	31/3/16		2/Lt Martin 7th Som L.I. ceased to be attached	

P.S. Norman Lt R.E.
for M.A.H. Scott
Capt R.E.
O.C. 814th Field Co R.E.

WAR DIARY or INTELLIGENCE SUMMARY.

(Erase heading not required.)

Army Form C. 2118.

84 FERE Vol 9

Place	Date	Hour	Summary of Events and Information	Remarks and references to Appendices
Camp 2m S.W. of ELVERDINGHE Sheet 28 A.26.b.7.3	1/4/16 to 16/4/16		3 & 4 Sections in Dugouts on Canal Bank working on left Bde area on front line work making connected trench along whole front.	
	6/4/16 & 7/4/16		1 & 2 Sections relieved 3 & 4	
	15/4/16		Company relieved on Canal Bank by 83rd Co R.E. who handed over to 12th Co.	
	16/4/16		Company relieved in Back Billets & entrained at HOUPOUTRE for CALAIS.	
	17/4/16 to 25/4/16		Company at CALAIS doing practice schemes in water supply, demolition & repair of bridges (theoretical) bridging & derricks. Also generally refitting & Drilling.	
	26/4/16		Marched CALAIS to billets near ZUTKERQUE	
	27/4/16		" from Billets near Z to VOLKERINCKHOVE	
	28/4/16		" V to HERZEELE where rested	
	29/4/16 30/4/16		In billets at HERZEELE Drilling	

30/4/16

M A H Scott
Capt R.E.
O.C. 84th Co R.E.

DAG
3rd Echelon

Herewith war
Diary of the 84 Field Coy RE
for the month of June and
July 1916. Regret this was
for many reasons not sent
away before owing to
oversight

M W Wilson
Capt
OC 84 Field Coy RE

1-7-16.

WAR DIARY or INTELLIGENCE SUMMARY.

(Erase heading not required.)

Army Form C. 2118.

Vol 10.
11.
May
June

Place	Date	Hour	Summary of Events and Information	Remarks and references to Appendices
HERZEELE	1/5/16		All available Sappers proceeded to L8 defences to improve works. 800 Iny attached returning night of 11th-12th. Remainder of Company at HERZEELE Resting & instructing Infantry of Brigade.	
	12/5/16			
	13th		Horse Show (Divisional)	
	14th		Instruction class for 60th Bde Officers & NCOs. Company drilling.	
	15th		On 15th O.C. + Advanced party with Lt Warde moved to take over Back Billets 75th Co at A 28 d 6.2 (Sheet 28)	
	16th		Advanced party went round Left Brigade area (Duke St to Pratt St in front of YPRES)	
YPRES	17th		2 Sections 3rd Company marched to Back Billets & proceeded to forward billets in YPRES on 18th	
	18th			
	19th		Remainder of Company marched in to back billets. 75th Co marched out.	
	20th		No 2 Section marched up to forward billets.	
	21st to 31st		Working on New trench B10a, wiring, Communication trenches, back wiring KAAIE Salient & MG Emplacements. On 27/5/16 No 1 Section relieved No 2. also 61st Bde relieved by 59th Bde.	

M Hson
Capt R.E.

WAR DIARY or INTELLIGENCE SUMMARY.
(Erase heading not required.)

Army Form C. 2118.

Place	Date	Hour	Summary of Events and Information	Remarks and references to Appendices
YPRES	1/6/16 to 30/6/16		On night of 2nd heavy shelling billets in YPRES hit but no damage. On night of 3rd No 4 Section relieved No 3. On night of 10th No 3 " relieved No 2. On night of 12th/13th raid on the mound which was unsuccessful. The infantry found the mound destroyed by fire of artillery & came back without any identification of force opposite. Sapper party with explosives, 2nd Lt Earl & six men never got into lines owing to infantry retiring at once. Casualties 2nd Lt Earl wounded in foot before starting, Cpl Suncombe at duty Sapper Cornall evacuated. Special firesteps used. On night 17th No 2 Section relieved No 1. On 24th inst. 2nd Lieut Norris joined 84th Co from 96th Co R.E. On night 25/26th raid on Salient very successful. Lt Manisty & 4 Sappers took over 4, 30 lb charges of ammonal. Destroyed 2 dugouts & an O.P. captured 4 prisoners. Lt Manisty repulsed counter attack. Casualties: Sapper Rhodes killed, Lt Manisty & Sapper Edmonds wounded. All ranks behaved with great coolness. Searchlight used successfully to show direction of return. Lt Hill directed searchlight. On 30th 2nd Lt Glover joined 84th Co from Base. Searchlight personnel went to base on 4th. Wagon & horses on 1st July & searchlights to be handed in on 2nd July to Ordnance. Special work done. Wiring WIELTJE trench & 21 ms special firesteps used.	

84th FIELD COMPANY R. E.

JULY 1916

20th Divisional Engineers.

WAR DIARY or INTELLIGENCE SUMMARY.

Army Form C. 2118.

July
84
84 F C R E
Vol 12

Place	Date	Hour	Summary of Events and Information	Remarks and references to Appendices
YPRES	1/7/16 to 5/7/16		Steel helmets have saved several lives & are very efficient. On night of 1st No 4 Section relieved No 3 Section. On night 4th/5th New CAVAN trench was dug. On morning 5th inst handed over to 96th Field Co R.E. & took over duties of back Company, i.e. all communication trenches KAAIE Salient, X line &c. No 2 Section went to Back Billets.	
	5/7/16 to 10/7/16		Worked as back Company on above works also work at VLAMERTINGHE + Dvnl H.Q.	
	10/7/16 to 15/7/16		Rest in Back Billets at H 28 D 6 2 (Sheet 28) near POPERINGHE	
LA CLYTTE	15/7/16 to 23/7/16		Marched to billets (Sheet 28) N.1.a.8.3 to work on O.Ps for 5th Corps leaving for HONDEGHEM on 23/7/16 (18 mile march).	
	24/7/16		Rest at HONDEGHEM	
	25/7/16		Marched to BAVINGCHOVE Stn + left at 9.57 am. for DOULLENS. Arrived at Stn at 6.30. Started entraining at 7.10 finished at 7.40 am. This is the shortest time the Coy have entrained in. Arrived DOULLENS at 2.30 pm & marched to HALLOY	
HALLOY	25/7/16 to 26/7/16		Rest at HALLOY	

WAR DIARY
or
INTELLIGENCE SUMMARY.

(Erase heading not required.)

Army Form C. 2118.

Instructions regarding War Diaries and Intelligence Summaries are contained in F. S. Regs., Part II. and the Staff Manual respectively. Title pages will be prepared in manuscript.

Place	Date	Hour	Summary of Events and Information	Remarks and references to Appendices
~~21/7~~ BALLOY	26/7/16 to 28		Marched to BUS-LES-ARTOIS & billetted in tents & huts with 61st Bde. 27th rested.	
	28th	morning	Marched to COURCELLES (2 Sections to COLINCAMPS & horses to ROSSIGNOL Farm. Took over billets from 157th Co R.E. & work from 123rd F Co R.E.	
	28th to 31st		Work in line mainly deep dugouts & clearing pre-trenches & firestepping the same. Line from K35a55.90 to Q4b5n.6. Sheet 57D.	

M G H Scott
O.C. 84th Co R.E.

84th FIELD COMPANY R. E.

AUGUST 1 9 1 6

20th Divisional Engineers.

84th Field Coy RE

WAR DIARY or INTELLIGENCE SUMMARY

(Erase heading not required.)

SECRET

Army Form C. 2118.

84 F.R.E.
Vol 13

Place	Date	Hour	Summary of Events and Information	Remarks and references to Appendices
COURCELLES	1/8/16		Back billets in COURCELLES forward billets COLINCAMPS. Work in Sector K33a 55.90 to Q4b 5.6 Sheet 57D mainly on Deep dugouts clearing fire trenches &c, handed over to 253rd Div. on 7/8/16 the whole Company moving to ROSSIGNOL Farm where the transport was on 7th inst. Adv party of No 1 Section proceeding there on 6th inst to erect huts.	
	7/8/16			
ROSSIGNOL FM	8/8/16 to 17/8/16		Working in yard supplying material for 83rd & 9th Co RE. Two sections putting in Gas Boxes in front line on 59th Bde Front. On 15th inst work ceased preparatory to moving on 17th inst.	
	17/8/16		Marched from ROSSIGNOL FM to THIEVRES & billeted there	
	18/8/16		Marched from THIEVRES to HEM & billeted there till 20th	
	19/8/16		Transport started march to MORLANCOURT via MERICOURT.	
	20/8/16		Dismounted personel marched to CANDAS Stn & entrained for MERICOURT then marched to MORLANCOURT rejoining transport there & billeting	
	21/8/16		Marched from MORLANCOURT to HAPPY VALLEY & camped there the night	
	22/8/16		Marched to position F12 c 6.9 (Old British trenches near CARNOY) & took over bivouac ground from 103 Co RE work from 104 Co RE. left Bde area in front. Work recovering trenches a little Deep dugout work &c.	
	27/8/16		61st Bde & 84th Co RE went into reserve. 84th Co with DLI started new	

Place	Date	Hour	Summary of Events and Information	Remarks and references to Appendices
F12 c 6.9 Sheet 62 D	27 8/16 to 31 8/16		New jumping off trenches for attacking GUILLEMONT. On night 26-27th Lt E.M GLOVER was wounded in leg & Lt WINBY rejoined the 84th Coy. Night of 30/31 still digging new jumping off trenches assisted by 2 Coys DLI.	

M A H Scott
Capt R.E.
O.C. 84th Co R.E.

84th FIELD COMPANY R. E.

SEPTEMBER 1916

20th Divisional Engineers.

20 Div
84 Field Coy RE
September 1916
Vol. 14

WAR DIARY or INTELLIGENCE SUMMARY

Army Form C. 2118.

Place	Date	Hour	Summary of Events and Information	Remarks and references to Appendices
F12 c 6.9 sheet 62D	1 9/16		On nights of 31/1st, 1st/2nd & 2nd/3rd working on gridiron increasing size & remaking the parts levelled by shell fire during the day. Work stopped early on morning 3rd to enable men to get back, breakfast, rest & get into position on Western edge BERNAFAY WOOD by 10.30am.	
	3 9/16		Day of the attack on GUILLEMONT. 84th Coy in reserve with 2 Cos 11th DLI. 20th Divn were successful but Divn on left 7th Divn not being able to hold GUINCHY our final objective was GUINCHY – WEDGEWOOD RD. Moved off about 4pm, the whole company carrying wire also the 2 companies DLI & wired the whole Divnl Front turning back the left flank along GUILLEMONT–COMBLES Ry. Casualties for the day 1 O.R.	
			On afternoon 4th the infantry were to take up a line from S.W. corner of LEUZE Wood to pt on Railway about ⊥ by strong patrols. The company on night 4th/5th moved up to dig strong pts on this line. Found the Right Bde had not sent out patrols but No 1 Section advanced & dug a post near QUARRY to S.W. LEUZE Wood. No 2 helped consolidate Front Line, No 3 helped patrols of Left Bde dig 3 small posts astride GUILLEMONT–COMBLES Rd & No 4 made a strong point near left of the line very near where the enemy were entrenching. Casualties: Lt Norris (No 4 Sect) & 1 O.R. wounded.	
	5 9/16		Rested at F12 c 6.9.	
	6 9/16		Marched to SANDPITS near MEAULTE & rested there till 8th inst.	

# WAR DIARY or INTELLIGENCE SUMMARY

Army Form C. 2118.

Place	Date	Hour	Summary of Events and Information	Remarks and references to Appendices
SANDPITS to MERICOURT	8/9/16		Marched with 61st Bde to MERICOURT L'Abbé billetted there the night.	
			2 Lt KOHL joined the Company in billets on night of 8/9/16.	
	9/9/16		Marched from MERICOURT to VAUX sur SOMME & bivouaced between VAUX & CORBIE T 19 c 7 sheet 62D	
	10 & 11		pontooning & bathing in the SOMME & lakes by it.	
	12/9/16		Marched with 61st Bde to bivouac at SANDPITS near MEAULTE about F 19 b 2.2. & remained there till evening of 14th inst. Drilling &c.	
	14/9/16		Marched to CITADEL & rested the night moving off without kit or coats &	
	15/9/16		3 days rations at 6.15 am 15/9/16 proceeding via TALUS BOISSÉES to WATERLOT FM. where we were in reserve to Guards Divn.	
	16/9/16		Moved up behind 61st Bde who were lent to Guards Divn & attacked on right of Guards. No 2 Section in Reserve. Heavily shelled all day but very few casualties. No 1, 3, & 4 Sections (Lt Hill, Warde, KOHL) advanced about 6 pm & consolidated the final objective reached by 61st Bde. Particular attention was paid to Left Flank which were in the air Guards not being able to reach objective. Line taken was approx T 9 d 3.7 to T 9 b 40.95	

WAR DIARY or INTELLIGENCE SUMMARY

Army Form C. 2118.

(Erase heading not required.)

Place	Date	Hour	Summary of Events and Information	Remarks and references to Appendices
WATERLOT FM.	17/9/16		Spent morning resting & then moved to BERNAFAY WOOD where we bivouaced.	
BERNAFAY WOOD	17/9/16 to 19/9/16		Made dugouts for staff, canteen, signallers. On night of 18th in consultation with 62nd Bde to settle left flank & 59th Bde for our right flank we dug a new bit of trench T26.9.1 to about T26.6.5. Heavy rifle firing by enemy. On 19/9/16 we returned to billets at CITADEL & rested 20/9/16 & 21/9/16	Casualties 3 OR killed 4 OR wounded
MEAULTE	22/9/16		On 22/9/16 we marched to BILLETS in MEAULTE where we rested till 25/9/16. Bathing, inspection of kit, cleaning wagons &c	
CITADEL	25/9/16		Marched to CITADEL F15c9.4 Sheet 62D.	
MALTZHORN VALLEY	26/9/16		Marched to MALTZHORN VALLEY 5.30 a, afterwards returning to A5a.	
	23/9/16		No 3 Section detached for work on CARNOY - ~~~~ FRICOURT and MARICOURT - BERNAFAY roads under CE 14th Corps. Section rejoined 27/9/16	
	27/9/16			
	27/9/16		Nos 1, 2 & 4 Sections employed on making dry weather track from	

WAR DIARY or INTELLIGENCE SUMMARY.

Army Form C. 2118.

Place	Date	Hour	Summary of Events and Information	Remarks and references to Appendices
CARNOY	27/9/16		T19 d 4.4 to T20 b 8.8. Company marched to CARNOY & took up billets at A15 c 2.2 with transport at A16 a 7.1	
CARNOY	28/9/16		Company rested	
LONGUEVAL	29/9/16		Company less part HQ transport moved to LONGUEVAL S16 d 8.2 in readiness to take over the line from RE of 62nd Inf brigade on night 29/9/16 – 30/9/16.	

A. Russell

J. Grosvenor Capt RE
act/OC 84th Fld Co RE

84th FIELD COMPANY R. E.

OCTOBER 1916

20th Divisional Engineers.

Vol 15

84th Field. Coy.

SECRET

WAR DIARY
or
~~INTELLIGENCE SUMMARY.~~

(Erase heading not required.)

Army Form C. 2118.

Place	Date	Hour	Summary of Events and Information	Remarks and references to Appendices
LONGUEVAL	1/10/16		On the 30th ulto the B.G.C 61st Brigade ordered six parties each of 1 NCO & 5 Sappers to report to CO.s 7th DCLI & 7th S.L.I. which batt's were holding the front line, 7th DCLI on left. 3 Parties under Lieut Kohl reported to CO 7th DCLI at 11.30 am 1st inst & 3 parties under Sgt Smith reported to CO. 7th S.L.I at 11.30 a.m. These parties were ordered to go forward after Infantry patrols & help them to consolidate. On the right the Sappers went forward at dusk and assisted in Consolidation without Casualties. On the left the Sappers (also Section M.G. Co) went forward with the Infantry, after advancing about 400 yards they came under M.G. & rifle fire & after taking cover in shell holes they were bombed out & had to retire to their original line, they reformed & advanced again about 250x & dug in. Casualties 2. O.R. missing 5. O.R wounded. 3 Sections R.E. & 1 Company 11th D.L.I. (Pioneers) joined up the Butts made by patrols ~~during the afternoon~~, the front line now runs approximately Sunken Road N 27 a 4.0 — a 7.2 — b 4.3 — b 7.2 — b 8.0	

WAR DIARY or INTELLIGENCE SUMMARY.

Army Form C. 2118.

(Erase heading not required.)

Place	Date	Hour	Summary of Events and Information	Remarks and references to Appendices
LONGUEVAL	Cont.d 2/10/16		N27 a 9.8 - N28 c 1.8 - c 3.6 - c 3.3	
"	3/10/16		One Section working on Cookhouses at Div HQ BERNAFAY WOOD	
"	4/10/16		Three Sections one 1 Coy DLI dug 370 yards assembly trenches behind front line. 61st Brigade relieved by 59th Brigade	
"	5/10/16		Three Sections working on Tracks East of TRONES WOOD and construction of Splinter proof RAMC Dressing Station at N.W. Corner BERNAFAY WOOD	
"	6/10/16		Company rested. 61st Brigade relieved 59th Brigade in front line	
"	7/10/16		4 Sections occupied ROSE TRENCH at 5 a.m. 61st Brigade attacked at 1.45 pm & captured RAINBOW & CLOUDY Trenches, RE went forward at 5 pm & consolidated, returned to billets 4 am Casualties 1 O.R. Killed 5 O.R. wounded	
MARICOURT	8/10/16		Company moved to Transport lines at MARICOURT	
"	9/10/16		Company moved to MEAULTE & took up old billets	
MEAULTE	10/10/16		Company rested	
	13/10/16		Corps Commander inspected Brigade + R.E. Congratulated the Bde on its achievements & appearance on parade. Congratulated O.C. 98th Coy personally on the appearance of the Company	

WAR DIARY or INTELLIGENCE SUMMARY.

(Erase heading not required.)

Army Form C. 2118.

Place	Date	Hour	Summary of Events and Information	Remarks and references to Appendices
MEAULTE	14/10/15		Training while at MEAULTE in explosives, wiring, Lectures to sections. Drill.	
	15/10/15		Marched to CORBIE with the 61st Bde group & were billetted there till 18th. Carried on drill, physical drill, rifle exercises, lectures &c.	
CITADEL	18th		Left CORBIE & proceeded by lorry to CITADEL F.15.c.9.4 sheet 62D. Transport proceeded by road leaving pontoons & cycles at MEAULTE dump & joined Company that night.	
A.2.d.5.0 ALBERT Sheet	19th		Marched to A.2.d.5.0 leaving transport at CITADEL for purpose of erecting huts. Erected huts till morning of 25th inst. Lt HILL acting Adjutant from 25th inst.	
	25th		Dismounted men with reinforcements of 83rd & 96th Companies proceeded by Bus to CONDÉ for training.	
CONDÉ	26th to 31st		Transport rejoined on 26th having marched. Training in trench digging, a little wiring, explosives &c. Hampered by lack of material for revetting, wiring &c.	

M. A. H. Scott
Capt R.E.
O.C. 84th Field Co R.E.

84th FIELD COMPANY R. E.

NOVEMBER 1916

20th Divisional Engineers.

SECRET WAR DIARY ~~INTELLIGENCE SUMMARY~~
(Erase heading not required.)

Army Form C. 2118.

[Stamp: 28 NOV 1916 — No. 84th FIELD COY. ROYAL ENGINEERS]

Vol 16

Place	Date	Hour	Summary of Events and Information	Remarks and references to Appendices
	November 1916			
CONDÉ (sheet 11 sq 6a)	1st to 7th		84th Coy with recent reinforcements of 83rd & 96th Coys attached carried out training programme consisting of wiring, trench revetting, setting out of trenches by day & by night, use of spars, suspension bridge, Weldon trestle, Explosives. Original sappers employed on notice boards & sundry jobs for CRE & 61st Inf Brigade.	
BERTANGLES	8th		No 1 Section (old sappers) moved to BERTANGLES to erect huts for R.F.C. Men by Bus	
ALLONVILLE	8th		No 2 " " — ALLONVILLE — — — — RFC — — —	
PICQUIGNY	8th		HQ & No 3 & 4 Sections with reinforcements from 83rd & 96th Field Coys & from No 1 & 2 Sections moved to billets at PICQUIGNY to continue training programme arranged for CONDÉ.	
PICQUIGNY	13th		84th Field Coy, with 11th DLI & 2 Battalions of 59th Inf Brigade inspected by General Rawlinson, Commanding 4th Army.	
LALEU	14th to 17th		84th Company less Nos 1 & 2 Sections moved to LALEU, area occupied by 61st Bde Group, continued work on Notice boards &c for 61st Bde & practiced use of Prismatic compass by night. No 1 & 2 Sections rejoined on the evening of 16th	

WAR DIARY

Army Form C. 2118.

Place	Date	Hour	Summary of Events and Information	Remarks and references to Appendices
LAHEU	18th		Dismounted personnel moved by Busses to DAOURS. Mounted & transport moved to ARGOEUVES & continued on	
	19th		19th to DAOURS.	
DAOURS	19th to 27th		No 1 Section detailed to continue construction of School for 17th Div. No 2 — — — — — — — — — 14th Corps Artillery No 3 — — — — — — — — — 20th Div No 4 — — — — — — — — — 29th — All this work had previously been in the hands of 29th Div RE who had been withdrawn from the Area some days previous to our arrival. Difficulty experienced by us in making progress owing to lack of material.	
CITADEL	27th		Company marched from DAOURS to the CITADEL spending night of 27th there	
MANSEL CAMP	28th to 30th		Company marched from CITADEL to MANSEL CAMP & started work hutting continuing work of 222nd F.C. R.E. & 1st H.C. Field Co R.E. who left on 27th inst. Lt CARROLL joined company on 6th inst leaving on 26th to join 54th Field Co R.E. 2/Lt DELAMAIN joined on 2nd inst & 2 Lts BIRD & TONKINSON joined on 19th inst	M.G.H. Scott Capt R.E.

84th FIELD COMPANY R. E.

DECEMBER 1 9 1 6

20th Divisional Engineers

SECRET

WAR DIARY or **INTELLIGENCE SUMMARY**
(Erase heading not required.)

84 Field Coy R.E.

Army Form C. 2118.

Vol 17

Place	Date	Hour	Summary of Events and Information	Remarks and references to Appendices
MANSEL Camp	1/12/16		At MANSEL Camp erecting Nissen huts, cookhouses latrines stables &c + making camp roads.	
	11/12/16		Omitted from last month Cpls Davidson & Ross & Cpls Handley & Booker received the Military Medal also Serjts Rust & Kerley (left the company when wounded) received the same on old recommendations	
	11/12/16		Marched to camp on GUILLEMONT Road east of TRONES WOOD S.30.a.7.7 & took over work from West Riding Field Company. Work mainly building Drying rooms cookhouses, latrines for standing Camps near GUILLEMONT maintenance of Duckwalk Drying rooms for front line Battns Tea & Soup kitchen, strong points & giving supervision + assistance to T.M. Batteries & M.G. Coys in erection of Dugouts also to 3 Field Ambulances in erecting Nissen huts for their Camps	
	23/12/16			
	23/12/16 to 31/12/16		Relieved by 93rd F.Co R.E. & marched to billets at MEAULTE taking over work from 77th Co R.E. Work two Sections at MORLANCOURT erecting sheds for hangars, 1 Section GROVETOWN on Corps rest station, remainder working on Corps Schools, MEAULTE Huts, Y.M.C.A. Hut, Church army huts &c at MEAULTE	

War Diary

of the

84th Field Company, R.E.

January 1917

Vol 18

SECRET

WAR DIARY or INTELLIGENCE SUMMARY.

Army Form C. 2118.

Instructions regarding War Diaries and Intelligence Summaries are contained in F. S. Regs., Part II. and the Staff Manual respectively. Title pages will be prepared in manuscript.

(Erase heading not required.)

Place	Date	Hour	Summary of Events and Information	Remarks and references to Appendices
MEAULTE	1/1/17		HQ + 3 Sections at MEAULTE one Section at MORLANCOURT building hangars for No 9 Squadron R.F.C. This section rejoined 4/1/17	
"	2/1/17		Company moved forward to relieve the 76th Field Co. HQ + 3 Sections at COMBLES, one Section + all transport at WEDGWOOD. 2 parties of Infantry from 61st Inf Bde attached for duty - 65 O.R. in all. 1 Section and all attached Infantry under the orders of GOC Left Brigade Group. 3 Sections under CRE. One Section employed on deep dugouts for MGs. One Section fitting bunks into dugouts made by 183rd Tunnelling Co. One section on Strong Point + MGE Brigade front U2C01 to U14b38 Sheet 57cSW4	
	3/1/17		Major M.A.H. Scott awarded Military Cross in New Years Honours List.	
	8/1/17		No 1 Section relieved by No 2	
	14/1/17		No 3 Section " " No 1	
	15/1/17		Capt Wade awarded Military Cross for Service rendered on Oct 7th /16 when in Command of No 3 Section opposite GUEDECOURT.	

WAR DIARY or INTELLIGENCE SUMMARY.

(Erase heading not required.)

Army Form C. 2118.

Place	Date	Hour	Summary of Events and Information	Remarks and references to Appendices
COMBLES	20/1/17		Major M.A.H. Scott left for LE PARCQ for Course of Instruction. No 3 Section relieved No 4.	
	18/1/17		2nd Lt Delamain & 2 O.R left for Course of Instruction at 20th Div School at DAOURS.	
	20/1/17		All work in hand Stopped & 3 Sections attached Infantry. 3 Companies of 11th D.L.I (Pioneers) 96th Field Co + one Section 83rd Field Co. R.E. employed on digging a new support line on Right Bde front from BREAD Trench to CAMEL LANE.	
	26/1/17		Company relieved by 77th Field Co R.E. No 3 Section went to DAOURS to work on 20th Div. School. No 2 Section went to No 9 Squadron R.F.C. to put up hangars + huts (at MORLANCOURT)	
GROVETOWN	31/1/17		Nos. 1 + 4 Sections with Coy H.Q. & transport went to GROVETOWN to put up huts for 34 C.C.S. + XIV Corps rest camp.	

Geo H Kyle
2 Lt R.E.
a/for 84 Field Coy R.E.

WAR DIARY

84 Fd Coy RE
Vol 19

Place	Date	Hour	Summary of Events and Information	Remarks and references to Appendices
GROVETOWN	1/2/17 6/2/17		Nos 1 & 4 Sections at GROVETOWN erecting huts &c for 34th C.C.S + XIVth Corps Rest Stn. No 3 Section at DAOURS working on R.A. + 20th Divl Schools with a few men at HEILLY working on 38th C.C.S; this Section marched to MORLANCOURT on 6th inst. No 2 Section at MORLANCOURT putting up hangars for 9th Squadron R.F.C.	
BERNAFAY WOOD S.29.C.	7/2/17 7/2/17 to 28/2/17		No 2 Section to CARNOY to take over D.O. R.E. duties from Officer of Kent F Co R.E. Rest of Company relieved Kent Field Co R.E. (No 498) + is in reserve. Work on back camps stables repairing frost damage to pipes & boilers &c. On night of 16th/17th relieved 83rd Co R.E. in right or MORVAL Sector. No 1 & 3 Sections going to advanced billets in Dugouts in BOVRIL Trench behind MORVAL + ½ No 4 to Left Bn HQ working on dugout there + helping infantry in Front + Support Lines. Work Dugouts + MG Emplacements On 20th inst ½ No 4 Section went to Forward Billets in BOVRIL Trench to work on MGEs On night 22nd/23rd Lts Bird + Belloc made reconnaissance for new trench in Left Bde Sector (LES BOEUFS Sector) These trenches were	

WAR DIARY or INTELLIGENCE SUMMARY

laid out by them & dug by D.L.I on night 24th/25th.

On afternoon 25th Lt Bird temporarily transferred to 96th Co for work owing to shortage of officers in 96th Co R.E. (probable duration 4 or 5 days)

On 27th inst party sent back to DAOURS to collect pontoons & cycles parked there returning on 28th inst.

During the month : Lt E.B. Tonkinson was struck off the strength being invalided to England.

" Lt G A Gibson was struck off strength on posting to 119th Ry Co R.E.

Lieut Schon temporarily transferred to 82nd Co R.E. was invalided to Base

28/2/17

Countersigned
A Bird Lt Major
a/c 2i/c

28/2/17

M. A. H Scott
O.C. 84th Co R.E.

WAR DIARY

~~INTELLIGENCE SUMMARY.~~

(Erase heading not required.)

84 FD Co R.E.

Army Form C. 2118.

Map ALBERT 57C

Vol 20

Place	Date	Hour	Summary of Events and Information	Remarks and references to Appendices
BERNAFAY WOOD S 29 c.	1/3/17		HQ & 1 Section & all transport. Two & half Sections at T 16 a 7.7 Half Section at T 12 a 6.9. One Section remaining with HQ employed on additions & repairs to Camps. Two & half Sections employed on deep dugouts M.G. emplacements &c Half Section employed on T.M. emplacement "2 Lt Willmott E.O.R. joined for duty from Base ROUEN	
S 29 c.	12/3/17		All Company together refitting bathing &c	
	13/3/17		"2 Lt Bellow" evacuated sick.	
BOVRIL	15/3/17		Three Sections moved to BOVRIL Trench T 16 a 7.7	
TRANSLOY	16/3/17		Two Sections moved forward to Cellars in LE TRANSLOY employed on examination of dugouts &c	
"	19/3/17		Third Section ditto	
"	20/3/17		Fourth Section ditto , all employed on road repairs, removal of Road Mines Booby Traps &c	
"	25/3/17		"2 Lt Bird T.F. reported at Infantry School FLEXICOURT for Course of instruction	
	28/3/17			

Place	Date	Hour	Summary of Events and Information	Remarks and references to Appendices
	night 28/29		61st Bde took NEUVILLE + on evening of 30th reconnaissance made by 2/Lt Willmott	
LE TRANSLOY	30/7/3		No 3 Section moved forward to Billets in BUS. Company still working on roads clearing new Dugouts, removing explosives &c.	

M. A. H Scott
Major R.E.
O.C. 84th Field Co R.E.

WAR DIARY
or
INTELLIGENCE SUMMARY.
(Erase heading not required.)

Army Form C. 2118.

84 Fd Coy R.E.

No 21

Place	Date	Hour	Summary of Events and Information	Remarks and references to Appendices
YTRES	1/4/17		Company less transport moved in YTRES from LE TRANSLOY & BUS. H.Q. at about P.20.d.8.8. changed to P.26.A.85.90 owing to shelling. Work on roads, clearing cellars dugouts &c & removing road mines. Also putting up billets for a Battalion in VALLEZART WOOD with derelict timber. Billeting work done in METZ, YTRES, NEUVILLE, BUS & ROYAULCOURT during the month. Strong points also dug & wired & forward tracks completed. Divisional HQ Billets in LITTLE WOOD built also of derelict timber felt & small quantity of weather & inch boarding. 84th was reserve company from night of 19th-20th till night 25/26th. Transport moved to YTRES on 27th. N°1 section moved to ROYAULCOURT on 26th N° 2 on 27th and HQ & other 2 sections on 28th inst. Work mainly billeting, searching road mines & dugouts, Siting reserve line & communication trenches	

M. A. H Scott
Major R.E.
O.C. 84 Fd Co R.E.

WAR DIARY or INTELLIGENCE SUMMARY

Army Form C. 2118.

84 Fd Coy RE
Vol 22

Place	Date	Hour	Summary of Events and Information	Remarks and references to Appendices
ROYAULCOURT	1/5/17		H.Q + 2 Sections at ROYAULCOURT + Transport at YTRES. Two sections moved into HAVRINCOURT Wood on 1st to make tunnel Dugouts for Batt. HQ 61st Bde holding left of Divisional Front with flank resting on CANAL du NORD. On night 4/5th 61st Bde advanced front on left to K32c 7.4 – K32 a 5.7 (Map 57C) One section under Lt K342 went to assist in revetting trench + wiring line across Slag Heap in K32. Revetting impossible that night owing to difficult digging but was done subsequently. General work in this sector: Making Coy. HQ's in Support line 5 in number, Batt. HQ's 3 in number (deep Dugouts) MG shelters splinterproof, wiring Reserve line + Support line in places hutting + running water supply. A footbridge put across Canal du Nord on night 7th/8th	
	11th		One section under Capt Norman with 1 Section 96th Co R.E. + Divl Hutting Section proceeded to SEVE Wood D21c (Sheet 62C) for Building New Divl HQ. Returned 15th inst. 60th Bde who should have relieved 11th about 12th inst, took over part of the line from 8th Divn. Divl front being extended to include LA VACQUERIE (61st Bde on left 59th Bde centre + 60th Bde on right) 40th Divn being on Divl Right. On a date unknown 48th Divn relieved 11th Divn on our left	
	19th		Whole Company assembled in YTRES being relieved in Line by 427th Coy R.E. belonging to 127th Bde 42nd Divn.	

WAR DIARY or INTELLIGENCE SUMMARY

Army Form C. 2118.

Place	Date	Hour	Summary of Events and Information	Remarks and references to Appendices
YPRES	20th		Company marched with 61st Bde to LE TRANSLOY camping at about O.27.c cent (Sheet 57C)	
	21st		Company marched " " " to FAVREUIL to relieve 15th Aust. Field Co. R.E. HQ at H.16 cent. thus commencing relief of 5th Aust. Divn.	
	21st to 28th		Company in Reserve with 61st Bde. 24th inst 59th Bde took over Right Bde area with 48th Divn on Right of them. " 60th " " " Left " " " 58th " " Left of them Divnl Front U.23.c.8.0 (Sheet No. 51B) to D.15.61.9 (Sheet 57C)	
	26th		61st Bde relieved 59th Bde in Right Bde area (front C.6 cent. to D.15.61.9) 84th Relieved 96th Field Coy with HQ and 3 Sections at C.29.a.4.2 Work deep dugouts + increasing accommodation, MG emplacement.	
	31st		Lt Bird went on leave 12/5/17. C.S.M Green & Sapper F.R. Green were mentioned in Despatches. L Cpl Craig killed on 26/5/17 by shell fire. In addition 5 O.R. struck off Strength + 4 joined.	

M A H Scott
Major R.E.
O.C. 84th Field Coy R.E.

WAR DIARY or INTELLIGENCE SUMMARY

824 Fd Coy R.E.
Vol 23

Place	Date	Hour	Summary of Events and Information	Remarks and references to Appendices
LAGNICOURT BEUGNY ROAD	1/6/17		HQ & 3 Sections living in sunken Road C.29.a.4.2 Sheet 57 C NW taping & spitlocking 2nd line on Right Brigade front. 1½ Sections on Deep dugouts for Batt. & Coy HQ & MG Crews with Infantry working parties	
FAVREUIL	1/6/17		Transport & Reserve section	
	5/6/17 6/6/17		59th Bde relieved 60th Bde in left Sector of Divl Front	
	8/6/17		Major Scott on Leave to UK 8th to 18th, ordered to report to W.O. on 10th inst	
	13/6/17 14/6/17		60th Bde relieved 61st Bde in Right Sector, 82nd Coy relieved by 83rd Coy RE.	
FAVREUIL	15/6/17		1 Section on general work in FAVREUIL, 3 Sections training	
	16/6/17		Major Scott struck off the Strength, Capt Norman appointed to command the Company with Acting rank of Major	
	21/6/17 22/6/17		61st Bde relieved 59th Bde in left Sector 8th Infy relieved 96th Infy Bde at NOREUIL C10C9.1	

WAR DIARY or INTELLIGENCE SUMMARY

Army Form C. 2118.

Place	Date	Hour	Summary of Events and Information	Remarks and references to Appendices
NOREUIL	23/8/17		3 Sections employed on Dugouts for Batt. Coy HQ & MG Emplacements & dugouts. One Section & HQ at FAVREUIL	
	22/8/17		Lt Belloc on leave to UK	
	22/8/17		Lt Kohl appointed 2nd in command with acting rank of Captain	
	25/8 26/8		No 3 Section from FAVREUIL employed on 2nd line digging posts	
	25/8/17		CSM Green appointed acting RSM. Sergt Rust " " CSM	
	27/8/17		61st Bde relieved by 186th Bde (62nd Division)	
	28/8/17		5th Field Co relieved by 457th Field Co	
	28/8/17		Coy inspected by CRE xx Div Lt Col Rolland DSO	
BIHUCOURT	28/8/17		Marched to BIHUCOURT G 11 d 8.1	
	30/8/17		Coy transport less water cart moved by road to ACHEUX (G.G Map LENS 11) 3 OR joined 4 OR struck off strength	

J. Thurman Major RE
OC 5th Field Coy RE

WAR DIARY
~~INTELLIGENCE SUMMARY~~
(Erase heading not required.)

Army Form C. 2118.

84 Fd Coy RE
Vol 24

Place	Date	Hour	Summary of Events and Information	Remarks and references to Appendices
BIHUCOURT (LENS 11)	1/7/17		Dismounted portion ~~of 84 Fd Coy RE~~, entrained at ACHIET-LE-GRAND and detrained at CANDAS, marched to billets at BERNAVILLE, transport joined unit from ACHEUX (less water cart which joined on 2nd)	
BERNAVILLE	3/7/17		Started 3 week training programme, drill, mounted & dismounted, Map reading, use of compass, Route Marches, Musketry, 20 rounds per man on 200x range at ~~WARNE~~ MT. RENAULT FM, visual training bombing & Lewis gun instruction, 4 days pontooning at LA CHAUSSÉE (AMIENS 17)	
	5th		from 9th - 13th inst. Company inspected by G.O.C. xx Div. on 5th inst	
	9-13			
	18th		& by CRE (Lt Col Newall RE) on 18th	
	13th		Divisional Horse Show. Company won - 2nd with Tool Cart, 3rd RE Jumble 4th Mounted NCO, 2nd prize for pontoon wagon & team divided with 83rd Field Coy RE.	
	21st		Company Marched to DOULLENS & entrained for GODWAERSVELDE (HAZEBROUCK 5A). Marched to E.4.c.8.1 (Sheet 27) PROVEN AREA	
HANDEKOT	16th		2 Officers and 152 R attached from Battalions of affiliated Inf Bde. for carrying during future offensive operations. "Lt Glover 7th KOYLI and "Lt O'Hagan 12th Kings L'pool Regt.	
	22nd to		Training continued, also forward area reconnoitred. Attached Infantry & Chinese Labour employed on construction of swimming bath on the	

Place	Date	Hour	Summary of Events and Information	Remarks and references to Appendices
ABANDEKOT E4c8.1 thus 27	27/7 26/7 3/7 15/7		HEIDEBEKE ponts at E3d9.1 works commenced on 26th 48 Stretcher bearers joined from battalions. Attd Inf Strength now 2 Officers 106 OR Church Parade. 4 Sappers put under instruction as Stretcher bearers. Training, hose respirators, making joints & laying Demolition charges. No 1 Section & attached infantry employed on baths OC on leave to UK 9th to 19th inst 2/Lt S.T. Spencer RE joined from Base 1 OR transferred 7 OR evacuated sick 4 OR joined

Thurman Wijn R.E.
OC 94th Field Coy R.E. | |

… DIARY
or
INTELLIGENCE SUMMARY.
(Erase heading not required.)

Army Form C. 2118.

84 Fd Coy RE

Vol 25

Place	Date	Hour	Summary of Events and Information	Remarks and references to Appendices
HAANDEKOT E4c8.1 Sheet 27	1/8/17 to 5/8/17		Work continued by Coy and attached Infantry on Swimming baths at E3d9.1.	
	6/8/17		61st Inf Brigade relieved 115th Inf. Bde in the line E of PILCKEM (Left Brigade front) Company moved to CANAL BANK C19c2.6 Sheet 28 & relieved 124th Field Coy RE. Dismounted personnel entrained at PROVEN & detrained at ELVERDINGHE. Transport proceeded by road to B30a3.6 Sheet 28. Work taken over. NIC.	
CANAL BANK C19c2.6	7/8/17		4 Sections + att'd Infantry employed 4 reliefs of 6 hours each on Extension of WINDSOR CASTLE Railway (Decauville)	
	8/8/17		Work handed over to Coy in Reserve (96th Field RE)	
	8/8/17 to 15/8/17	incl.	Coy + att'd infantry employed making a mule track from (C8a8) to C3b2.9 (E of PILCKEM). Weather very unsettled which necessitated using hard wood planking in places where shell holes had been filled in. Work only possible at night & shelling frequently heavy, particularly gas shelling which delayed work considerably. Track through for pack animals on the 12th inst. Traffic of 3 Brigades pack transport very heavy, causing a large amount of repair work to be done. Pontoon waggons employed bringing up hard wood slabs which were laid to make track possible for wheeled traffic. This was only about 50% complete by the night of the 15th inst.	

WAR DIARY or INTELLIGENCE SUMMARY.

Army Form C. 2118.

Place	Date	Hour	Summary of Events and Information	Remarks and references to Appendices
CANAL BANK C.19.C.2.6	16/8/17		20th Div attacked at 4.45 a.m. with 61st Bde on left, Northern boundary BOESINGHE - STADEN Rd, Southern boundary PILCKEM - LANGEMARCK Road, 60th Brigade on Right & 59th Brigade in reserve. 600x tracing tape laid out on Brigade front 125x behind Barrage line, (E of R. STEENBEKE) by OC and Capt. Kohl R.E. on XY night. Nos 2, 3 & 4 Sections employed under Bgde making Strong Points, 2 behind 1st Objective & 2 on 2nd Objective, work commenced 2 hours after Zero & continued until 3 p.m. parties heavily shelled most of the day & hostile MG fire prevented any work being put out in daylight. As no Counterattack developed during the night, conditions were much more favourable for R.E. Consolidation after dusk. No.1 Section & attached Infantry employed under CRE. to make bridge the STEENBEKE on PILCKEM-LANGEMARCK Road, party arrived about noon. Enemy endeavoured by shell fire and MG fire from Aeroplanes to prevent any work being done, 2nd Lt Allanson N.C.O. i/c Job wisely decided that a bridge would be destroyed before dusk, decided to use his material in constructing a large box Chain & making a ford possible for Field guns, this was completed successfully by 6pm, a very fine piece of work under difficulties.	
	17/8/17		Company relieved in CANAL BANK by 123rd Field R.E, moved	

WAR DIARY or INTELLIGENCE SUMMARY

Army Form C. 2118.

(3)

Place	Date	Hour	Summary of Events and Information	Remarks and references to Appendices
P5 Area (PROVEN)	17/8/17		to MALAKOFF F⁰ Camp B.22 central Sheet 28	
	18/8/17		1 O.R. & all Infantry entrained at ELVERDINGHE, detrained at PROVEN marched to E.17 d.5.3 Sheet 27. Transport by road.	
	19/8/17		Resting.	
	20/8/17		Repitting Tool Carts, Cycles, Kit & Equipment. C⁰y prepared for Inspection by C in C, inspection cancelled.	
	21/8/17		GOC 20th Div. called to congratulate C⁰y on excellent work done during previous fortnight.	
	23/8/17		No 4 Section proceeded by lorry (transport by road) to B.14.c.4.3. (Sheet 28) ELVERDINGHE to build new Divisional HQ	
	24/8/17		14th Corps Commander (Earl Cavan) called & congratulated the Company on previous fortnights work. Nos 1, 2 & 3 Sections, HQ & transport joined No 4 Section	
	25/8 to 31/8		Work on new Div HQ, roads & huts. Casualties for the month Joined. 2/Lt L. Belloc. wounded (gas) Lt Col E. Morris RE TF Spencer — H. Wilman RE R of O. 14 OR wounded (includes 5 Wounded-at Duty) 11 OR 11 OR gas 15 " Evacuated Sick	

A.S. Norman
Major RE
OC 84 Field Co/RE

WAR DIARY or INTELLIGENCE SUMMARY

(1) 84 Fd. Coy R.E.

Vol 26

Place	Date	Hour	Summary of Events and Information	Remarks and references to Appendices
WELSH F.m ELVERDINGHE	1/9/17		HQ, 4 Sections & 100 Attached Infantry employed building new Divisional HQ Camp, NISSON Huts, roads etc.	
	10/9/17		HQ & 3 Sections & attached Infantry moved to CANAL BANK C19 a 0.7 (Sheet 28 NW) transport moved to B 23 d 9.1. No 2 Section remained at WELSH F.m to complete Camp. Coy relieved 123rd Field Co R.E. 20th Div relieved 38th Div in right Sector 14th Corps front.	
	11/9/17 to 17/9/17		Coy employed digging reserve line (GREEN LINE) running across Divisional front from U 22 d 8.2 to N 29 b 35.30 (Sheet 20)	
	16/9/17		No 3 Section relieved No 2 at WELSH F.m	
	18/9/17		Coy took over duckboard track from 96th Field Co R.E. track runs from PILCKEM to REITRES F.m & beyond parallel to BOESINGHE – STADEN Rly formation, Also work on duckboard track for right Brigade running from PILCKEM to S of LANGEMARCK	
	20/9/17		20th Division attacked with 59th & 60th Brigades; 61st Brigade in reserve. Coy employed extending 2 duckboard tracks forward on night of 21st	

WAR DIARY or INTELLIGENCE SUMMARY

Army Form C. 2118.

Place	Date	Hour	Summary of Events and Information	Remarks and references to Appendices
CANAL BANK C.19.a.0.7 sheet 28.	21/9/17 to 24/9/17		3 Sections employed on maintenance & extension of duck-board track, extension of accomodation of Brigade HQ & Sleeping Strong point in front line	
	25/9/17		No 3 Section moved to SIEGE Junction (B.20.d.5.8 sheet 28) to construct Horse lines for Brigade winter quarters	
	25/9/17 to 28/9/17		2 Sections employed on Duckboard track from Bridge 6 to EAGLE TRENCH & erecting notice boards in forward area	
	29/9/17		20th Div relieved in front line by 4th Div. 84th Field Co relieved by 9th Field Co RE. Company moved to P.5 Area with HQ at E.17.d.6.3.	
	30/9/17		Co rested	

H.J. Thomson Major RE
OC 84th Field Co RE

WAR DIARY
or
~~INTELLIGENCE SUMMARY~~
(Erase heading not required.)

Army Form C. 2118.

84 Fd Coy RE
Vol 27

Place	Date	Hour	Summary of Events and Information	Remarks and references to Appendices
PROVEN Sheet 27	1/10/17		Company & attached Infantry moved from P.S Area (PATAGONIA Camp) to HOPOUTRE entrained there 11 pm, detrained at BAPAUME 2 pm 2nd	
BAPAUME Sheet 57c	2/10/17		Company marched to billets at YTRES	
YTRES Sheet 57c	3/10/17		Company rested	
	4/10/17		Company marched to billets at HAUT ALLAINES (62c)	
	5/10/17 to 7/10/17	incl	Training. rifle & box respirator drill, Kit inspection	
SOREL (Sheet 57c)	8/10/17		Company & attd Infantry marched to billets at SOREL-LE-GRAND	
HEUDECOURT	9/10/17		Company moved to HEUDECOURT & relieved 224th Field Coy RE (40th Div) in the line. Nos 3 & 4 Sections moved forward at night to advanced billets in VILLERS GUISLAIN (sheet 57c), & took over forward work in right Brigade area of Left Division 3rd Corps. 59th Brigade on left & 55th Div on right. 61st Brigade holding line from R 27 a 7.6 (N of GONNELIEU, & 300x S of main PERONNE - CAMBRAI Road) to X 11 a 0.6 Sheet 57c SE. Brigade holding 3400x frontage with 2 batts in line one in close support & 1 in Reserve.	
	10/10/17 to 31/10/17		Nos 3 & 4 Sections & attd Inf employed on deep dugouts, MG emplacements trench maintenance & drainage. Nos 1 & 2 Sections & attached inf employed erecting huts in back area Brigade horse Lines etc also Reserve batt Camp	

Place	Date	Hour	Summary of Events and Information	Remarks and references to Appendices
HEUDECOURT. Sheet 57C	31/10/17		Casualties
Lt C.V.E. Morris R.E. transferred to Area Employment (? 3rd Army) 19/10/17
2/Lt F.H. Martin R.E. joined for duty 26/10/17
Capt G.H. Kohl wounded 27/9/17
1 O.R. wounded
4 O.R. to hospital (Evacuated)
21 O.R. joined from Base

[signed] Thomson
Major R.E.
O.C. 84th Field Coy R.E | |

WAR DIARY

Army Form C. 2118.

Place	Date	Hour	Summary of Events and Information	Remarks and references to Appendices
HEUDECOURT Sheet 57c	1/11/17 to 6/11/17		HQ + Nos 1 & 2 Sections + att^d Infantry employed in HEUDECOURT Area building shelters & camps. Nos 3 & 4 Sections billeted at VILLERS GUISLAIN and employed on MG emplacements, water supply, & trench maintenance & drainage.	
	7/11/17		No 3 Section returned to HEUDECOURT. Employed on construction of details Camp for 61st Inf Brigade. No 1 Section employed constructing one battalion bivouac camp under camouflage at W 4 C (Sheet 57c) which proved to be quite invisible from the air. No 4 Section employed hutting at Main Dressing Station & RAILTON Camp. No 2 Section + attached Infantry returned to HEUDECOURT	
	18/11/17		Rest & packing up of transport, pontoons etc	
	19/11/17			
	19/11/17	3 pm	No 3 Section moved forward to fix Artillery Bridges (23 No) over our front support line trenches on Div front.	
	20/11/17	4 am	No 2 Section moved forward & came under orders A.G.C. 61st Inf Bde. They were ordered at 11 am to construct 2 strong points

WAR DIARY

Army Form C. 2118.

Place	Date	Hour	Summary of Events and Information	Remarks and references to Appendices
	20/11/17		N & NE of VACQUERIE (Sheet 57 C) which were completed during the day without difficulty.	
	20/11/17	6 a.m.	No 3 & 4 Sections with att'd Inf all Tool Carts & pack animals moved forward to VILLERS PLOUICH. Remainder of Transport except pontoon Section moved forward to VILLERS PLOUICH 1 p.m.	
	21/11/17		Nos 1 & 2 Sections employed clearing sunken roads (part only) from VACQUERIE to MASNIERES.	
	25/11/17		Nos 3 & 4 Sections employed wiring MLR NE of LATEAU WOOD (12th Div front). 700x of fence & double apron erected	
	22nd 25th 11/17		No 1 Section moved forward to dugouts in HINDENBURG Line at R 9 b 3.2. Sheet 57 C	
	25/11		No 2 Section moved forward to join No 1.	
	26/11		No 1 & 2 Sections moved to dugouts in L 34 b 1.3. Sheet 57 c	
	27/11		Nos 1 & 2 Sections & att'd Inf employed digging MLR from M 3 a 6.5 to G 33 b 2.8. (61st Inf Brigade front) Sheet 57 b.	
	28/11			
	30/11			

WAR DIARY or INTELLIGENCE SUMMARY

Army Form C. 2118.

Place	Date	Hour	Summary of Events and Information	Remarks and references to Appendices
	27/11/17		No 3 Section employed digging M.L.R. with Nos 1 & 2 Sections	
	28/11/17		No 4 Section employed making Rear Billets & horse standings in VILLERS PLOUICH	
	29/11/17		Nos 3 & 4 Sections employed constructing duckboard track along sunken road from VACQUERIE to MASNIERES.	
			Casualties	
	29/11/17		Lt Hill RE attached for duty. Lt Ewlett to hospital, Sick.	
	24/11/17		4 Lt F. H. Martin RE Killed	
			1 O.R. Killed	
			5 O.R. wounded	
			3 O.R. to hospital Sick (Evacuated)	
			4. Horses (R2) Killed by shell fire	

Thomson Major RE
O.C. 2nd Field Coy RE

WAR DIARY or INTELLIGENCE SUMMARY

(Erase heading not required.)

84 Fd Coy R.E.
Vol 29

Army Form C. 2118.

Place	Date	Hour	Summary of Events and Information	Remarks and references to Appendices
	1/12/17		Movements of Company & attached Infantry during period Midnight Nov 29th to Midnight Dec 3rd recorded in Appendix A attached. J. Browne Major R.E. O.C. 84th Field Coy R.E.	
HURLU	3rd	Midnight	4 Sections HQ & all transport billeted at HURLU (Sheet 57C) under orders to move at 8 a.m. Dismounted personnel by Bus to BUIRE & transport by road to MEAULTE (AMIENS Sheet 1)	
	4th		Dismounted personnel proceeded to BUIRE by bus arriving 10.0 p.m. and transport by road to MEAULTE arriving 6.0 p.m.	
	5th		Portion of transport moved off at 5.0 p.m. and arrived at ORVILLE at 2.0 a.m. by road with 61st Infantry Brigade transport. Moved off at 11.0 a.m. and reached BOUBERS at 5.0 p.m.	(LENS Sheet 11)
	6th		Dismounted personnel with remainder of transport moved by rail, entraining at AVELUY to HESDIN and on by road to CREQUY arriving 6.30 a.m.	
	7th		Left CREQUY at 1.0 p.m. and arrived at HENOVILLE 3.0 p.m. Portion of transport left BOUBERS 9.15 a.m. and arrived at ECQUEMICOURT at 4.0 p.m.	(CALAIS Sheet 13) (ABBEVILLE Sheet 14)
	8th		Portion of transport left ECQUEMICOURT at 9.0 a.m. and joined remainder of Company at HENOVILLE at 2.0 p.m.	

WAR DIARY or INTELLIGENCE SUMMARY

Army Form C. 2118.

Place	Date	Hour	Summary of Events and Information	Remarks and references to Appendices
	9/12/17 to 11/12/17		Company resting, bathing, re-equipping and drilling.	
	12/12/17		Dismounted personnel left HENOUVILLE by bus at 10.30 a.m. and arrived at 4.0 p.m. in BLARINGHEM area with H.Q. at F.4.2.4. Transport moved by road to THIEMBRONNE arriving 3.0 p.m.	(HAZEBROUCK Sheet 5 A)
	13/12/17		Transport moved off at 8.0 a.m. and rejoined remainder of company at 6.30 p.m. (23 miles)	
	14/12/17		Transport moved to STAENEELE	
	15/12/17		Transport moved to RE farm N.14.d.9.2 (Sheet 20) near KEMMEL via BAILLEUL	
	16/12/17		Remainder of company moved by bus to same camp	
	18/12/17		Company working on IX Corps defence line zone on Right Divisional Sector under CRE 20th Division under orders of Corps. Scheme including several belts of wire, M.G. posts and cover and strong points.	
	19/12/17 to 25/12/17		Continued carriage of wiring materials by horsed transport to forward dumps and along line of wire by carrying parties. Width of front to be wired 4,200 yards. Severe frost prevented erection of wire. All wire carried and formed into 100 yard dumps along line by 25/12/17.	
	26/12/17		Severe weather continued but wiring was commenced, each picket hole having to be prepared by pick.	

Place	Date	Hour	Summary of Events and Information	Remarks and references to Appendices
	27/12/17 to 30/12/17		Continued wiring Corps line and reconnaissance work in area	
	17/12/17		Major P.G. NORMAN M.C. R.E. mentioned in Despatches
Corp. T. HORSFALL " " "
Major P.G. NORMAN on leave to England 5/12/17 - 20/12/17
Lt. H. MILLMAN R.E. " " " " 21/12/17 - 4/1/18
Lt. E.A. EARL R.E. " " " " 29/12/17 - 12/1/18
Lt. T.F. PORTER R.E. joined for duty from Base 5/12/17

Casualties
1. O.R. killed
6. O.R. wounded
6. O.R. evacuated sick
19. O.R. joined company

H. Ellis Hill
Lt. R.E.
a/tt 84 Fld. Coy. R.E. | |

WAR DIARY or INTELLIGENCE SUMMARY.

Army Form C. 2118.

APPENDIX "A" (1)

Place	Date	Hour	Summary of Events and Information	Remarks and references to Appendices
			Recording Movements of 1st Field Co. & attached Infantry during German attacks; covering period Midnight Nov 29th to midnight Dec 3rd referred to in War Diary attached.	
Dugouts S. of MARCOING L.34.b.1.3	30/11/17	8.45 a.m.	Nos 1 & 2 Sections & att'd Infy. were in dugouts having returned from digging on M.L.R at about 11 pm previous night. It was reported to me that a large number of wounded were coming back also stragglers & that it was rumoured that the Germans had broken through our front line defences along the Canal between MASNIERES and South Eastwards. Immediately reported to Brigade Major 61st Brigade (L.34 central) who ordered me to stand to & man attd. HINDENBURG system near Brigade H.Q. In moving into position I met the B.G.C 61st Bde who placed No 1 Section in trench about L.34.c.9.6. I placed No 2 Section & all stragglers available into trench (old C.T.) running NE from about L.34.d.0.5. to about L.34.d.25.70. At this time small parties of Germans could be seen about 600x E of the road running N & S through L.34 central, also large numbers of enemy moving down the slope (Cont'd)	

WAR DIARY or INTELLIGENCE SUMMARY.

APPENDIX A

Place	Date	Hour	Summary of Events and Information	Remarks and references to Appendices
	30/12/17		Northwestwards in R.12.c & R.18.a, from this I concluded that a further attack was imminent & proceeded to reconnoitre. On the right at about 234 c.4.4. I found an Officer & a few sappers of 83rd Field Coy RE & oddments of other regiments in an important trench & immediately sent up 20 men under a Sgt to reinforce. I then received information that Major Ray 7th DCLI required reinforcement & sent him 1 NCO & 70 men & a message that I would move up the remainder of my command if he required them.	
		10.30 am (about)	I met BGC 61st Brigade who informed me that his Bde Major was wounded & Staff Captain missing, & that I would take over the duties of Bde Major temporarily.	
		5 pm	I sent for 2/Lt J.E. Bird RE (OC No 2 Section) & gave him orders to collect Nos 1 & 2 Sections & move forward with them & report to Lt Col Janson, CO 7th KOYLI & come under his orders. The 2 Sections remained there until the 61st Bde was relieved by the 182nd Brigade at 2 am Dec 3rd when they moved back to NORLU under orders issued by 61st Brigade.	
NORLU	3/12/17	9.30 am	Nos 1 & 2 Sections arrived at billets in NORLU in an exhausted condition (Contd)	

WAR DIARY or INTELLIGENCE SUMMARY.

Army Form C. 2118.

APPENDIX "A"

Place	Date	Hour	Summary of Events and Information	Remarks and references to Appendices
VILLERS-PLUICH	30/11/17		Movements of Nos 3 & 4 Sections during period covered for Nos 1 & 2 Sections, reported to me after relief by Lt H.E. Hill R.E.	
		8 a.m.	Nos 3 & 4 Sections paraded 8 a.m. & moved through LA VACQUERIE to continue work on duckboard track in ~~Masnieres~~ LA VACQUERIE Valley toward MASNIERES.	
		8.30 a.m.	Lt Hill left VILLERS-PLUICH to join the sections & on his way forward learnt that the Enemy had broken through the 12th Div's front, he placed No 3 Section in trench CORNER WORK & No 4 in trench about R10c9.7 when he reported to Col Prior (? spelling) C.O. Battn of 59th Brigade who ordered him to bring No 3 Section forward to HINDENBURG Support Line & later (6 p.m.) ordered him to move forward again to HINDENBURG front Line & establish posts along it as far as R16b31.	
		7 p.m.	Lt Hill received a message that C.R.E. wished Nos 3 & 4 Sections withdrawn but Col Prior was unable to let them go until reinforcements arrived.	
		10 p.m.	A Battn Sherwood Foresters arrived & took over from Nos 3 & 4 Sections when they moved back to VILLERS-PLUICH.	(cont'd)

WAR DIARY or INTELLIGENCE SUMMARY

Army Form C. 2118.

APPENDIX A

Place	Date	Hour	Summary of Events and Information	Remarks and references to Appendices
VILLERS-PLUICH	30/11/17	11.30 pm	On arrival of Nos 3 & 4 Sections at Y-P they were ordered by CRE to occupy a trench overlooking FIFTEEN RAVINE	
	1/12/17	6 am	Nos 3 & 4 Sections ordered by G.S.O.1. 20th Div to occupy trench running from R19a 9.1 towards VILLERS-PLUICH	
	2/12/17	7 am	Nos 3 & 4 Sections (alongside sections of 83rd Field Coy RE) moved by orders of Major Massie OC 83rd Field Coy RE to occupy LINCOLN AVENUE S of and adjoining DUNRAVEN trench	
	3/12/17	1 am	Lt Hill received orders from G.S.O.1. to move back to NURLU	
NURLU	3/12/17	3.30 am	Nos 3 & 4 Sections arrived in billets.	

TRANSPORT

	30/11/17	9 am	Lines at R19d moved to METZ, less one double tool cart which was at L3c Central & had to be abandoned, portions of mounted Section (notably L/Cpl SPREADBURY & Cpl HORSFALL) did very good work in taking SAA up to the firing line under heavy shell fire. Pontoon equipment, bicycles & sundry other technical equipment had to be abandoned, also Cooks gear & some equipment of Nos 1 & 2 Sections	

J. Sherman
Major RE
OC 84th Field Coy RE

WAR DIARY or **INTELLIGENCE SUMMARY**
(Erase heading not required.)

17   84 Fd Coy R.E. Army Form C. 2118.

Vol 30

Place	Date	Hour	Summary of Events and Information	Remarks and references to Appendices
	1/4/18 to 3/4/18		Continued wiring Corps Line & reconnoitring new area.	
	4/4/18		Nos 3 & 4 Sections moved from R.E. FARM N.14.d.9.2 (sheet 28) to CANADA TUNNELS at I.30.a.5.0 sheet 28. - continued Corps Line wiring same night.	
	5/4/18		Nos 1 & 2 sections moved up & joined Nos 3 & 4 Sections & all four sections went out wiring Corps line. Hd Qrs & Transport moved to new lines at H.30.B.1-7.	
	6/4/18 to 12/4/18		All four sections employed putting up a double apron fence (2 belts) along 61st F.B. de front commencing from the Right Divisional Boundary at J.26.a.1-3, - (sheet 28) a total of 1800x (equivt Single belt) completed & material for same carried up, joined up to existing wire. This belt of wire known as "Reserve Line."	2 Sections R.E. (3 & 4) returned to billets at Inf1 (1 & 2 Sub) went forward to Canada Tunnels
	13/4/18		Work on No.7 Strong point, excavating & draining. No working or carrying parties.	
	14/4/18 to 18/4/18		Commenced wiring 3rd belt (double apron fence) to Reserve line, now called "Main Line of Resistance" 800x completed. No.7 Strong Point, draining, excavating revetting & sandbagging, work much impeded by weather, which alternated between snowstorms & thaws, necessitating much of the work on the S.P. being done twice. Nos 3 & 4 Sect + Att Infantry relieved Nos. 1 & 2 Sect Att Inf1, the latter returning from CANADA TUNNELS to Rear billets. Commenced sending up 1 sect R.E & Att Inf1 each afternoon from Rear billets for night work forward.	

WAR DIARY or INTELLIGENCE SUMMARY

Army Form C. 2118.

Place	Date	Hour	Summary of Events and Information	Remarks and references to Appendices
SCOTTISH WOOD H 35 b Sheet 28 NW	19/1/18 to 25/1/18		No 3 & 4 Sections working on Nos 6 & 7 Strong points respectively. No 1 & 2 Sections coming forward on alternate nights to wire M.L.R.	
	25/1/18		No 1 & 2 Sections relieved Nos 3 & 4, all 4 sections working forward on night of 25th inst. No 7 Strong point at J.26.a.9.9 renamed No 2. — No 6 S.P. at J.20.d.45.30 renamed No 3.	
	26/1/18		No 1 Section working on No 2 S.P. No 2 Section on No 3 S.P.	
	27/1/18		Working party 50 men L.I. dug No 1 S.P. at J.26.a.15.75 under No 1 Section. No 1 continued on No 2 S.P. No 2 on No 3 S.P.	
	28/1/18		No 1 Section revetting S.P. 1. No 2 Section working on S.P. 2. No 4 Section wiring Int. Line.	
	29/1/18		No 1 Section revetting S.P. 1 & 2. No 2 Section revetting S.P. 3, & supervising deepening of PALESTINE trench. No 3 Section wiring Int Line.	
	30/1/18		No 1 Section revetting No 1 S.P. No 2 Section on S.P. 3 & PALESTINE trench. No 4 Section wiring Intermediate Line.	

WAR DIARY or INTELLIGENCE SUMMARY

Army Form C. 2118.

Place	Date	Hour	Summary of Events and Information	Remarks and references to Appendices
HQ at SCOTTISH ND H 35 b Sheet 28 NW	31/7/18		No 1 Section wiring S.P.1 No 2 Section deepening PALESTINE Trench & converting STEVENS Trench J.20.d.75.25 for all round defence. No 3 Section wiring Intermediate Line. Casualties Lt A.E. Hill MC RE wounded 16/7. 2nd Lt E.C. Delamain RE Transferred to R.F.C. 9/7. Lt J.F. Porter wounded (Gas) 4/7. 2nd Lt L. Belloc joined for duty 6/7: 2nd Lt A.G. Peters joined for duty 13/7. 2nd Lt G. Brown joined for duty 24/7. 2nd Lt G.W. Montz joined for duty 26/7. 2 Officers & 100 O.R. Infantry from 61st Bde attd to Coy 11/7 for work 1 O.R. wounded (on duty) 3 O.R. joined Coy 12 O.R. Evacuated sick 53189 "Cpl Spreadbury F Awarded M.M. 1/7	

A.J. Brown Major R.E.
O.C. 84th Field Coy R.E.

WAR DIARY
or
INTELLIGENCE SUMMARY
(Erase heading not required.)

84th Field Co R.E.

Army Form C. 2118.

Vol. 31

Place	Date	Hour	Summary of Events and Information	Remarks and references to Appendices
SCOTTISH WOOD	1/2/18		HQ & Transport & Nos 3 & 4 Sections. Sections employed improving & extending Bns Battle at VIDJERHOEK & erecting huts, etc in back Area.	
H 35 b Sheet 28 NW			Nos 1 & 2 Sections billeted in CANADA TUNNELS I 30 a 5.0 Sheet 28 working on Strong points on M.L.R.	
	2/2/18		Nos 3 & 4 Sections relieved Nos 1 & 2 in forward area.	
	10/2/18		Nos 1 & 2 — — 3 & 4 — —	
	16/2/18		Coy relieved by 154th Field Co R.E. in forward area & by 155th Co in back area. ~~[struck through]~~ Coy transport moved to STRAZEELE under 7 Lt Mentz RE (Sheet HAZEBROUCK SA)	
	17/2/18		— — — — HEURINGHEM — — — —	
	17/2/18		Dismounted personnel entrained at DICKEBUSCH, detrained at EBBLINGHEM (dits) marched to HEURINGHEM	
	18/2/18		Rest	
	19/2/18 to 28/2/18 incl		Overhauling Technical Equipment, Kit etc. Drill, target practice (60d range)	

84th Field Co. R.E.

WAR DIARY or INTELLIGENCE SUMMARY

Army Form C. 2118.

(Erase heading not required.)

Place	Date	Hour	Summary of Events and Information	Remarks and references to Appendices
HEURINGHEM (Sheet HAZEBROUCK 5A)	21/2/18		Company moved to RACQUINGHAM (4 miles) & took over billets previously occupied by 83rd Field Co RE	
	22/2/18		Company moved to STEENBECQUE & entrained there during the afternoon. Detraining	
	23/2/18		at 6.30 a.m. at NESLE (Sheet AMIENS 17) Marched to billets at TIRLANCOURT (V16 Sheet 66D)	
	24/2/18		Rest	
	25/2/18		Section Drill, rifle exercises, practice in laying Demolition charges	
	26/2/18		Recreational training & practice with WELDON trestles	

Casualties Transfers

Lt. H. MILMAN RE transferred to RFC   7-2-18
Lt. L. BELLOC RE   "   "   15-2-18
2 officers 100 OR attached Infantry rejoined Units 15-2-18
Lt. G. PITT RE reported for duty   26-2-18
2/Lt. H.C. ASHWORTH RE "   "   10-2-18

WAR DIARY or INTELLIGENCE SUMMARY.

Army Form C. 2118.

Place	Date	Hour	Summary of Events and Information	Remarks and references to Appendices
TIRLANCOURT (sheet 66ᴰ)	28/2/18		Casualties & Transfers (cont'd) 1 OR died of wounds 10-2-18 2 OR wounded 15 OR joined from the Base 11 OR evacuated sick [signature] Major RE OC 94ᵗʰ Field Coy RE	

84th FIELD COMPANY R. E.

MARCH 1918

20th Divisional Engineers

WAR DIARY or INTELLIGENCE SUMMARY

(Erase heading not required.)

Army Form C. 2118.

84 Fd Coy R.E.
Vol 32

Place	Date	Hour	Summary of Events and Information	Remarks and references to Appendices
TIRLANCOURT (Sheet 66D)	1/7/18		Training	
	2/7/18		Ditto	
	3/8/18		Company moved as follows. N°1 Section to HAM, N°2 3 & THQ to CANIZY (Sheet 66D I.28) N°4 Section to VOYENNES (I.7 Sheet 66D). Dismounted personnel by lorries. Transport by road.	
CANIZY	4/8/18		Setting out of work on Green Line from HAM inclusive running Westward along SOMME CANAL to I.6.C.4.8 sheet 66D. with outpost line running about 1000 yds from centre of HAM on North side.	
	6/8/18		System of defence. outpost platoons at about 500" intervals with equal number of supporting posts 250" in rear. Counter-attack Companys 500" in rear of front outpost & 1 Company Redoubt about 1000" 1500" in rear each Battn Front 2000" each Battn Front having about 16 MGs.	
	7/8/18		2 Coys of Infantry (60th Inf Bde) & 2 Italian Labour Bns employed cutting brushwood in front of positions	

WAR DIARY or INTELLIGENCE SUMMARY

Army Form C. 2118.

(2)

Place	Date	Hour	Summary of Events and Information	Remarks and references to Appendices
CANIZY	8/3/18 and 9/3/18		2 Battns of 60th Inf Bde + 3 Italian Labour Cos (187th, 189th & 120th) employed on looking posts	
	10/3/18		2 Battns as above. COs placed under orders to be prepared to move at 2 hours notice	
	14/3/18		2 Batts (12 KRR + 12 RB) 3 Italian Labour Cos (120th 187th + 189th) employed digging on forward line. Barb wire fence + double apron erected	
	15/3		on front of about 1000x in front of HAM	
	16/3		Work as above also 21st Entrenching Battn employed	
	17/3		No work. 60th Inf Bde Horse Show. One entry in NCOs jumping	
	18/3		Work as on 16th. Two Field Engineers reported (Capt Potts RE & Lt Warner RE) to take over work in the event of Jt being withdrawn	
	19/3		Work as on 18th but one Coy 11th DLI (Pioneers) employed in addition to other units	
	20/3	2:30pm	COs warned to be ready to move at once	
		8:30pm	Test move carried out	
	21/3	6:30 am	COs ordered to move (warning order)	

WAR DIARY of INTELLIGENCE SUMMARY.

Army Form C. 2118.

(3)

Place	Date	Hour	Summary of Events and Information	Remarks and references to Appendices
HAM.	21/3	4 pm	Coy moved to ST SULPICE HAM. No 1 & 4 Sections reforming at 5.30 pm	
	21/3	6.15 pm	Orders received for 1 Section to join 61st Inf Bde at DURY. No 1 Section moved at 6.45 pm	
	21/3	8.30 pm	Orders received for remainder of Coy to join 61st Inf Bde. Coy moved at 9.15 pm to DURY. OC reported to 61st Bde Adv HQ at ST SIMON & received orders to move Coy from DURY to OLLEZY, arrived about 4 am	
	22/3	7 am	Received orders from BGC 61st Bde to reconnoitre line running from TUGNY-ET-PONT through Canal Junction just W of ST SIMON & Southwards towards ANNOIS & to employ 1 Coy (D) 11 DLI (Pioneers) on digging also all available Sappers. Pioneers ordered to report to CO 12th Kings (L'pool) Regt for work. OC held to reconnoitred line (on right) held by 7th Battn South L I & discussed it with CO Battn who agreed that on that line there were ample trenches for defence. German patrols came into contact with our Outposts on Canal at about 8.45 am	
		10 am	Reported result of reconnaissance to BGC 61st Inf Bde who	

WAR DIARY or INTELLIGENCE SUMMARY

Army Form C. 2118.

Place	Date	Hour	Summary of Events and Information	Remarks and references to Appendices
	22/3/18	10am	Ordered Coy to improve "GREEN" line defences, running due E of OLLEZY & SW of ST SIMON. Line was reconnoitred & found to be spit-locked practically throughout. Some small (listening) posts dug to depth of 5'. Coy commenced work at 11.30 am to cut firesteps in section posts & to dig additional posts as far as possible.	
		11am	Transport ordered by Staff Capt to move back to a point near where CUGNY-HAM road crosses Railway.	
		6pm	OC ordered by BGC to meet him & CO reserve Battn (7th DCLI) at Bde HQ 7pm & decide steps to be taken to improve defences of OLLEZY, which defences consisted of posts & were garrisoned by DCLI	
		7pm	Decided that all RE should be employed digging on that line with garrison up to midnight & that RE should then move back to transport lines to get some sleep & so be available for work on 23rd if required.	
		11pm	Received orders from Bde Major to repair a bridge across CANAL on	

WAR DIARY or INTELLIGENCE SUMMARY

(Erase heading not required.)

Army Form C. 2118.

Place	Date	Hour	Summary of Events and Information	Remarks and references to Appendices
	22nd		DURY - OLLEZY road which had been partially demolished for such by RE of another Formation detailed for the job	
		1.30pm	OC proceeded to DURY to left Battn HQ to see how Coy of Pioneers were employed & found them engaged as Infantry & CO reported them as not available for other work owing to the great length of line which his Battn were holding	
		11.30pm	Orders sent to Transport Lines for necessary Tools required for repair of Bridge to come forward on pack animals. No 4 Section detailed to commence work on Bridge at 12.30 am	
	23rd	2am	No 1, 2 & 3 Sections arrived at Transport Lines	
		7am	No 4 " " " " "	
		6am	OC received orders from BGC to report immediately	
		7am	OC reported to BGC at Pt S of OLLEZY near Railway & received instructions to employ "D" Coy 11" DLI on digging two redoubts in front line system S of Railway, also to site 5 MGs with OC MG Coy at points laid down by BGC	

WAR DIARY or INTELLIGENCE SUMMARY

Army Form C. 2118.

(6)

Place	Date	Hour	Summary of Events and Information	Remarks and references to Appendices
OLEEZY	23	10 am	Orders received from Bde Major to prepare bridge for demolition which had been repaired previous night by No 4 Section.	
		10.15 a	Wtn orders sent to Transport Lines with orders for Nos 1, 2 & 3 Sections to come forward immediately with necessary Tools & explosives for work. One Officer & 2 NCOs per section to come on ahead on cycles. Wtn orders never reached & 2 days later it was discovered that he had been stopped en route by a Unit of 36th Div, his horses taken from him & he given orders to man a trench with that Unit.	
		12	Transport moved to GUISCARD under Bde orders, also 4 Sections. Bde HQ moved to BROUCHY & shortly afterward to VILLESELVE	
		5 pm	Transport & 4 Sections arrived VILLESELVE. having been moved forward by Bde	
		7 pm	4 Sections to went forward to dig & occupy a line astride VILLESELVE — CUGNY Road about 300x E of VILLESELVE	
	24	11 am	4 Sections ordered to go forward & dig in & occupy 4 posts. 2 facing N & 2 facing E, all about 1000x E of MONTALIMONT Fm (W of CUGNY) they were to occupy these posts to enable the battalions	

WAR DIARY or INTELLIGENCE SUMMARY

Army Form C. 2118.

Place	Date	Hour	Summary of Events and Information	Remarks and references to Appendices
	24		forward to fall back on to them	
		3pm	Enemy advanced on left & right of our position very rapidly & threatened to envelope VILLESELVE & troops E of it, this was brilliantly countered by 8th Dragoons who charged Wood NW of VILLESELVE & brought back about 100 prisoners	
			From this period Enemy advanced so rapidly that it was impossible to keep in touch with events. Bde HQ had moved from VILLESELVE about 2pm & were not afterwards located though search was made in BEINES, BERLANCOURT, GUISCARD & later at SERMAIZE without success. Transport was moved by Bde during morning from VILLESELVE towards BERLANCOURT & later (about 10.30 a.m.) to ground 1 mile S of BERLANCOURT. About 12.30pm Transport moved (without orders from Bde) through GUISCARD to MUIRANCOURT as Infantry (French) were forming a line in rear of the transport lines.	
		6.30pm	QMS reported that he had been to FRENICHES to refill but while there had received orders to move immediately, he had received no orders as to there	

WAR DIARY or INTELLIGENCE SUMMARY

Army Form C. 2118.

Place	Date	Hour	Summary of Events and Information	Remarks and references to Appendices
	24		& when to refill, & was ordered by OC to join Bde HQ transport which was then in a field ½ mile E, to move & refill with them & to rejoin Cn at SERMAIZE that night. An officer was sent to NOYON to endeavour to get information as to location of HQ & time & place of refilling with orders to report to Cn at SERMAIZE by 10 pm & Mounted orderly sent to ROYE to locate 20th Div. trspt to Cn following a.m. at LASSIGNY. Both means proved unsuccessful. Cn Transport moved during the night to LASSIGNY with a view to refilling somewhere on railway running N&S. ROYE - RESSONS	
	25	12 noon	Arrangements were made by phone from ROYE-SUR-MATZ to refill at RESSONS-SUR-MATZ, transport was then approaching ROYE when information was received that Supply wagon had gone back. Emergency refilling arrangements were then cancelled & OC with transport billeted at CONCHY-LES-POTS when orders were received from CRS 20th Div to move to ROYE on 26th & thence to HANGEST-EN-SANTERRE	
	26	4.30 am	Orders received from CCS to move immediately to QUESNEL & billet as far W of ROYE as possible	

WAR DIARY or INTELLIGENCE SUMMARY.

(9)

Place	Date	Hour	Summary of Events and Information	Remarks and references to Appendices
	26	5.25pm	Fm moved to MEZIERES via ONVILLERS, FAVEROLLES, DAVENSCOURT, QUESNEL, FRESNOY-EN-CHAUSSEE arriving about 8pm	
	About	6pm	4 Sections refused transport	
		8pm	Orders received from CRE to attach one Section to 61st Inf Bde	
	27	7am	No 4 Section moved transport to 61st Inf Bde at BEAUFORT where OC Section received orders to dig occupy posts in support E of the village	
	27	11am	Orders received to employ all available Spr on digging a line between LE QUESNEL & HANGEST this was modified later & a line was dug S of HANGEST running towards PLESSIER	
	28		Orders received 5.30am to move to DOMART at 8am. fm started in rank & ordered to take up a spur E of HOOD SE of DOMART & await further orders	
		4.15pm	Orders received from CRE to move all transport to BOVES, this was altered & in rank & transport moved to SAINS-EN-AMIENOIS	
		10pm	Orders received for all Sections to move to billets at DOMART	
	29	1.15pm	Orders received from CRE to dig a line running NE & SW about 1000x E

WAR DIARY or INTELLIGENCE SUMMARY.

Army Form C. 2118.

(Erase heading not required.)

(10)

Place	Date	Hour	Summary of Events and Information	Remarks and references to Appendices
			cross roads DEMUIN – MOREUIL & AMIENS – ROYE. this was modified & at dusk Coy dug line just E of cross roads	
	30	7 am	Orders received from CRE to move to BOVES	
	31		Coy remained in billets at BOVES	
			Map Sheets ST QUENTIN 18, AMIENS 17	
HAM	21st		Bridging wagons & teams withdrawn from Coy by CRE	
	26th		" " " rejoined Coy at HANGEST	
	27th		" " " withdrawn by CO Divl Train & moved to ABBEVILLE	
			Experience gained during month has shown many objections to the practice of affiliating Fd Coys to Inf Brigades; before the battle ie from 1st to 20th of the month 16 orders were received of action to be taken in certain eventualities 11 by Div Bde & 5 by CRE in some cases these orders did not coincide; at the end of the first 12 hours of movement Coy was in its fourth billet & from then onwards Coy was employed in digging & garrisoning trenches. A Railway Arch (road under Railway) at OLEEZY. Several bridging wagons complete with bridging equipment & other	Sd Af

Place	Date	Hour	Summary of Events and Information	Remarks and references to Appendices
			Stores could have been destroyed or rendered useless if orders had been issued	
			Strength of Coy on 1st of month 7 Officers 205 O/R	
			Transfers Postings etc. 11 Lt G.W. Mentz R.E. to 503rd Field/R.E.	
			11 Lt H.C. Ashworth R.E. to 222nd " "	
			11 Lt C.B. Wigan R.E. joined for duty from Base 27-3-18	
			Lt Munn R.E. attached for duty 27-3-18	
			Lt Munn R.E. transferred to Foreways 31-3-18	
			Lt T.W. Leslie R.E. joined for duty from Base 14-3-18	
			2 O/R to Foreways 10-3-18 6 O/R joined from Base	
			Casualties Lt G. Pitt R.E. wounded 24-3-18	
			Lt A.G. Petrie R.E. " 27-3-18	
			O/R 1 Killed 14 Wounded 14 Missing 13 to hospital sick.	
			Strength of Coy on 31st inst 5 Officers 167 O/R	
			40701 Cpl Sincombe S.C. awarded DCM 28/12/17	

WAR DIARY or INTELLIGENCE SUMMARY.

Army Form C. 2118.

84th R.E. (?)

Vol 33

Place	Date	Hour	Summary of Events and Information	Remarks and references to Appendices
	1st		HQ + 2 Sections at BOVES (AMIENS Sheet 17) Transport at SAINS-EN-AMIENOIS	
	1st	3pm	4 Sections moved forward & dug a line of posts W. of GENTELLES	
		9pm	Embussed on AMIENS-ROYE Road NE of BOVES, debussed at	
	2nd		QUEVAUVILLERS 1am, marched to billets at FRESNOY-AU-VAL, transport moved from SAINS & rejoined at 1pm	
	3rd	3pm	Coy. moved to ST AUBIN-MONTENOY	
	4th	2pm	Coy. moved towards BEAUCAMPS-LE-JEUNE, DR met Coy en route with orders to return to ST AUBIN-MONTENOY	
	5th		Refitting wagons, cycles & kit.	
	6th		Training commenced. Medical Inspection by MO 1/1 R.E.	
	7th+8th		Training & refitting.	
	9th		Coy. moved to BROCOURT (DIEPPE Sheet J2)	
	10th		" " " LE PLOUY (ABBEVILLE Sheet)	
	11th		" " " OUST MAREST (" ")	
	12th		Cleaning Technical Equipment. Army Act Section 4 to 44 read.	

WAR DIARY or INTELLIGENCE SUMMARY

Army Form C. 2118.

(2)

Place	Date	Hour	Summary of Events and Information	Remarks and references to Appendices
OUST MAREST	12/4 to 16th		Training refitting Tool Carts & Equipment, Pontooning, Range firing 10 rounds per man at 100ˣ. 100 men bathed	
	17th		Transport except Limbers & water Cart & G.S.wagon moved 9.30 pm to PONT REMY arriving 10 am 18th	
	18th		Remainder of Transport & Dismounted personnel moved at 8.30 pm Entrained at EU (sheet ANCEVILLE)	
MARQUAY	19th		Detrained at TINCQUES & marched to MARQUAY (F2 Sheet LENS 11)	
	20th		Gun Transport repaired, Equipment cycles & wagons cleaned Ovens built &c	
	21st to 29th		Training Drill, Rifle exercises, Musketry instruction Schemes &c Defence of Localities, Demolition Schemes	
	30th		Moved to CAMBLAIN L'ABBÉ (LENS 11 Sheet)	

WAR DIARY or INTELLIGENCE SUMMARY

Army Form C. 2118.

(3)

Place	Date	Hour	Summary of Events and Information	Remarks and references to Appendices
CAMBLAIN - L'ABBE	30/4/18		Strength on 1st April 5 Officers 169 O/R.	
			Transfers	
			~~1 Lt Ha............~~	
			Lt V.G. HOLGATE RE transferred from 83rd Field Coy 8/4/18	
			1 Lt. G.E.A. GREENSILL RE joined for duty 24/4/18.	
			1 Lt. E.J. HOAR RE — — — 24/4/18.	
			Casualties	
			1 O/R wounded. 11 O/R to hospital sick.	
			Postings	
			47 O/R joined for duty from the Base	
			6 O/R previously reported missing, rejoined	

Signed
OC 86" Field Coy RE

84th FIELD COMPANY, R.E.
No. 1 Date: 31 MAY 1918

WAR DIARY or INTELLIGENCE SUMMARY.
(Erase heading not required.)

Army Form C. 2118.

84 Field Co
Vol 34

Place	Date	Hour	Summary of Events and Information	Remarks and references to Appendices
CAMBLAIN L'ABBÉ	1/5/18	9am	Orders received from CRE to relieve 7th Canadian Field Co with HQ at ABLAIN ST NAZAIRE. No 1 & 2 Sections less transport moved to adv billets at M29.C.7.6 & relieved two sections 7th Canadian Co on front N13b.7.0 Southbank to SOUCHEZ R. (LENS SECTOR)	
	2/5/18		No 3 & 4 Sections moved to S.6.b.4.2 & took over work & adv billets from 2 Sections 7th Field Co CE. (AVION SECTOR)	
ABLAIN ST NAZAIRE	2/5/18		Transport moved from CAMBLAIN L'ABBÉ & took over billets from 7th Canadian Co CE at ABLAIN ST NAZAIRE	
	3/5/18		No 3 & 4 Sections handed over work & billets in AVION SECTOR to 83rd Field Co & moved to rear billets	
	4/5/18		No 1 & 2 Sections employed on dugouts & trench maintenance. No 3 & 4 on making & maintenance of 4 road nears under road junctions around SOUCHEZ	
	1/5/18		No 3 Section relieved No 1 & 2 Sections at forward billets	
		10pm	Co warned to be prepared to Man Battle Stations at short notice. 84th & 96th Field Co detailed to Garrison ARTHURS SEAT (S.4. Sheet ST NAZAIRE RIVER). Trenches re-	

WAR DIARY or **INTELLIGENCE SUMMARY.**
(Erase heading not required.)

Army Form C. 2118.

84TH FIELD COMPANY, R.E.
No. 2
Date 3 1 MAY 1918

Place	Date	Hour	Summary of Events and Information	Remarks and references to Appendices
ABLAIN ST NAZAIRE	9/5/18		Connoitred during the night by Officers & again on morning of 10th inst.	
	16/5/18		2 Sections wiring A12.65. (N25a Sheet 36C SW1) 4 belts each 750" long	
	17th		fence & double apron. 2 Sections making Artillery tracks to forward area. Gas proofing dugouts. Maintaining 4 Road Mines & dismantling 2 hospitals & 4 ordinary NISSON huts.	
	11/5/18		No 4 Section moved to forward billets	
	18/5/18		No 1 & 2 relieved 3 & 4 Sections in forward area.	
	19/5/18 to 31/5/18		No 1 & 2 employed in digging new switch fire trench joining BLUE TO RED Line on left of Div Front. Constructing 1 deep dugout, trench maintenance, wiring out post Line. Construction of small (timber) shell proof shelters in Front Line.	
	19/5/18 to 28/5/18		No 3 & 4 Sections employed constructing Artillery Tracks, erecting & Nisson of 2 hospital NISSONS in ABLAIN ST NAZAIRE, erecting & repairing road screens, maintenance of 4 Road Mines in SOUCHEZ area	
	28/5/18		No 4 Section moved to join No 1 & 2 Sections for work in forward area	

WAR DIARY
or
INTELLIGENCE SUMMARY.
(Erase heading not required.)

Army Form C. 2118.

84TH FIELD COMPANY. R.E.
3
31 MAY 1918

Instructions regarding War Diaries and Intelligence Summaries are contained in F. S. Regs., Part II. and the Staff Manual respectively. Title pages will be prepared in manuscript.

Place	Date	Hour	Summary of Events and Information	Remarks and references to Appendices
	23/4/18		Company practised Manning Battle Stations on ARTHURS SEAT. Orders issued 1 a.m. All sections in position 3.43 a.m.	
	29/4/18		Lt. T.H. Leslie R.E. wounded (Gas)	
			Strength on May 1st. 8 Officers 208 O/R	
			Casualties	
			Killed 2 O/R	
			Wounded 1 Officer 2 O/R + 1 O/R wounded at duty	
			Missing Nil	
			To Hospital (Sick) 6 O/R	
			Joined from Base 9 O/R	
			Strength on 31st May 7 Officers 207 O/R	
			Extract from London Gazette dated 20/5/18	
			Mentioned in despatches	
			T/Capt (A/Major) R.G. Norman T/Lt F.A. Burl. D/- (Lcpl.) Bevan T. 32137.	R.G. Norman Major R.E. O.C. 84th Field Coy R.E.

84TH FIELD COMPANY, R.E.
3 0 JUN 1918

WAR DIARY or INTELLIGENCE SUMMARY

(Erase heading not required.)

Army Form C. 2118.

VR 35

Place	Date	Hour	Summary of Events and Information	Remarks and references to Appendices
ABLAIN-ST NAZAIRE (LENS II)	1/6/18		Nº 1, 2 & 4 Sections billeted in CITE DES GARENNES M.29.c.6.6. (Sheet 44) Employed in constructing shell proof shelters for garrison of forward trenches. Nº 3 Section HQ & all transport at ABLAIN ST NAZAIRE	
	5/6/18	3.25am	Orders received "Test Man Battle Stations" All Sections in position 4.50 am. Div'l Commander inspected Personnel & Transport at Rear Billets at 5.30 pm	
	6/6/18		Forward Sections relieved by 96th Field Coy RE. Whole Coy billeted at ABLAIN-ST NAZAIRE night 6th/7th	
	7/6/18		Baths & Cleaning up	
	8/6/18		All Sections employed building Rein Comp in ABLAIN-ST NAZAIRE accommodation for 3(?) (Station Hut) proceeded & job handed over to	
	14/6/18		93rd Field Coy RE to complete	
	16/6/18		Corps Bde Horse Show Coy won 4 first & 2 second Prizes	
	15/6/18		Nº 2, 3 & 4 Sections relieved 96th Field Coy RE in forward area	
	19/6/18		Sections employed on concrete OPs shell proof shelters MGEs	
	23/6/18		Took over Light power Rings at M.22.c.3.15.20 (Sheet 44)	

WAR DIARY or INTELLIGENCE SUMMARY

Army Form C. 2118.

84th FIELD COMPANY, R.E. — 30 JUN 1918

Place	Date	Hour	Summary of Events and Information	Remarks and references to Appendices
	24/6/18		No 1 Section relieved No 2 Section forward.	
	26.		No 1 & 2 od Sections employed on Concrete O.P. Platoon posts concrete shell proof shelters M.E.R.	
	30/6/18		Strength on June 1st	
			7 Officers 207 O.R.	
			Casualties	
			Wounded 3 O.R.	
			Evacuated Sick 9 O.R.	
			Joined Coy 12 O.R.	
			Strength on 30th June 7 Officers 207 O.R.	
			Major P.G. Rosman M.C. on leave to U.K. 24/6/18 – 8/7/18	
			Extract from London Gazette dated 6/6/18	
			Cpl Buckingham G.S. awarded D.C.M.	

R.G. Moffat Capt.
O/C 84 Field Coy R.E.

WAR DIARY
or
INTELLIGENCE SUMMARY

84 Fd Coy RE

Vol 36

Army Form C. 2118.

Place	Date	Hour	Summary of Events and Information	Remarks and references to Appendices
ABLAIN-ST-NAZAIRE (LENS II)	1/7/18		Sections No 1, 2 & 4 billeted at STAFFORD HOUSE (M22B.15.20 Sheet II) at work on Concrete OP Concrete platoon posts, Shellproof shelters & MGE. Heavy gas shelling on nights of 30/6/18 & 1st & 2nd inst. a fair number of casualties.	
	5/7/18 6		96th Field Co. took over work in forward area whole coy billeted at ABLAIN ST NAZAIRE night 5/6th	
	6/7/18		Baths & cleaning up.	
	7/7/18		All sections employed dismantling Old COLUMBIA camp + erecting it at X 3 D 2mm preparing range at MARQUEFFLERS	
	10/7/18		No 2 section commenced work on Reserve Bde HQ at M26D7.3.	
	14/7/18		No 1 & 2 Sections took over work in forward area from 96th Field Coy. New area bounded on South by LENS-LIEVEN Rd. Advanced billets in dugouts at M.15.D central. No 3 section at work on Reserve Bde HQ & No 4 section on Columbia Camp. Work on Shellproof shelters Concrete OPs	
	16/7/18		No 3 section came forward for work on Lewis Gun posts but as	

WAR DIARY ~~INTELLIGENCE SUMMARY~~

Army Form C. 2118.

(2)

Place	Date	Hour	Summary of Events and Information	Remarks
			cement available so worked on trenches and improvement of forward billets.	
	22/23	night	Raid by 6th Bde. Spr THOMSON J. & Spr HAWKINS E. went with 7th Seaf H¹ & Spr BOARDMAN E with Cornwalls. First two wounded at duty.	
	23/7/18		No 4 section relieved No 1 section forward.	
	31/7/18		No 3 Section returned to rear billets for work in back area.	
			Strength on July 1st 7 officers 207 OR.	
			Casualties.	
			Wounded 36 OR (gas)	
			" 2 OR (at duty).	
			Evacuated sick 11 OR	
			Joined Coy 37 OR	
			Lt T.W. LESLIE rejoined from hospital 23/7/18.	
			Strength on 31 July 8 officers 201 OR.	

J.S. Holgate Capt RE
for O.C. 2nd Field Coy

WAR DIARY ~~or INTELLIGENCE SUMMARY~~

(Erase heading not required.)

84 Fd Coy R.E.
Vol 37
Army Form C. 2118.

Place	Date	Hour	Summary of Events and Information	Remarks and references to Appendices
ANZAIN-ST NAZAIRE	1/8/18		HQ and No 1 & 3 Sections full transport at ANZAIN ST NAZAIRE (Sheet LENS 11) Sections employed on construction of NEW CORONGANS Bn Camp. No 2 & 4 Sections living in dugouts at M15 d.6 employed on work in forward area. 2 Concrete OPs for Artillery, concrete Lewis gun Posts & assisting Infantry in maintaining Line & Communication trenches in Bn Fr Bde Area.	
	3/8/18		No 1 Section relieved No 2 Section in Forward Area	
	4/8/18	10pm	"Test" Man Battle Stations ordered. All Sections in position 1.30 am returned to Billets.	
	12/8/18		No 3 Section relieved No 4 Section in Forward Area	
	22/8/18		Spr Goldstein, Dobson & Waissell attached to raiding party of 12th Kings L'Pool Regt. each carrying 1, 20 lb Mobile Charge (ammonal). 2 Charges were successfully used, third not required as the objective was found to have been destroyed by Heavy Artillery.	
	23rd		No 2 relieved No 1 Section in Forward Area	
	23/8		Adv Billet moved to ANGRES M33 d.5.70 owing to Div side-stepping one Bn front on Northern boundary, South in this area handed over to 103rd Fd Coy 28.	

WAR DIARY or INTELLIGENCE SUMMARY

Army Form C. 2118.

Place	Date	Hour	Summary of Events and Information	Remarks and references to Appendices
			(24th Divn) except Artillery OP in ST PIERRE which was continued by this Coy	
ABLAIN ST NAZAIRE	27/8		Coy relieved by 129th Field Coy (24th Divn) Left Bde of 20th Divn relieved by a Bde of 24th Divn. Coy billets at ABLAIN ST NAZAIRE night of 27/28.	
	28/8		Coy relieved 2nd Field Coy (8th Divn) HQ & 1 Section at LA TARGETTE A16.8.10 (Sheet 57B). 3 Sections in dugouts S.30.c.5.5. (Sheet 44A). Work in hand 2 water supply plants, 1 Electric light plant, construction of a new Dressing Station, shelters in Main Line of resistance & 4 strong points in Out Post Line of Resistance. Front taken over T.16.a.2.9. to T.28.2.5.6. (about 2500x front)	
	29/8		Work continued by new Section on hut camp at ABLAIN ST NAZAIRE	
	30/8		Rev Section training. Lt. T.W. Leslie RE sick to Base 6/8/18. 1 Lt. BEA Transill RE & 8 S/R proceeded to MATRINGHAM to 1st Army Musketry Meeting 12th-16th inst. Team took 17th place of 49 Competitors. 1 Lt G. Brown RE granted Leave to UK 16th - 30th Lt J.E. Bird RE " " " " 27th - 10th	

WAR DIARY
or
INTELLIGENCE SUMMARY.
(Erase heading not required.)

Army Form C. 2118.

Place	Date	Hour	Summary of Events and Information	Remarks and references to Appendices
LA TARGETTE	31/8		Lt McBrid RE to hospital 14th to 20th inst.	
			Inf Officers attached for 10 days instruction in RE work	
			" Lt Halpin 7th DCLI 2nd to 16th inst.	
			" Lt Barker 7th SLI 20th to 31st	
			6 NCOs granted 10 days leave to Paris	
			Div RE Horse Show 17th inst Coy awarded 1st for pontoon wagon team	
			2nd - Tool Cart	
			Maj MacArthur to Coy XX inst	
			VII Corps Horse Show 24th Coy awarded 1st for pontoon wagon team	
			244216 Spr TRICKETT A awarded Military Medal 11/8/17 for good	
			work done in a raid on enemy lines on night of 30/31st July	
			Strength of Coy on Aug 1st 8 Officers 201 O/R	
			Casualties 1 Officer wounded sick	
			1 O/R killed	Strength Aug 31st 7 Officers 208 O/R
			2 wounded	
			9 sick	A. Sherman
			Reinforcements joined 19 O/R	Major RE OC 94th Field Coy RE

WAR DIARY
~~INTELLIGENCE SUMMARY~~
(Erase heading not required.)

Instructions regarding War Diaries and Intelligence Summaries are contained in F. S. Regs., Part II. and the Staff Manual respectively. Title pages will be prepared in manuscript.

Army Form C. 2118.

84TH FIELD COMPANY, R.E.
No. ....
Date 30 SEP 1918

VR 38

Place	Date	Hour	Summary of Events and Information	Remarks and references to Appendices
LA TARGETTE (LENS II)	1/9/18		HQ & No. 1 & 3 Sections at LA TARGETTE. No 4 Section employed on NEW COLUMBIA Camp, building Cookhouses roads etc. No 3 Section Training. Nos 2 & 4 Sections at Advanced billets on LENS ACROSS Road 1 mile N of VIMY employed on running pumping & lighting engines, maintenance of water mains & tanks, construction of A.D.S. & trench shelters & drainage.	
	3/9/18		No 2 Section withdrawn to Rear billets.	
	4/9/18		No 2 - employed on work on Camps No 1 & 3 on 7 days intensive training	
	12/9/18		No 1 relieved No 4 at Forward billets.	
			No 3 relieved No 2 - rear billets	
	13/9/18		Nos 2 & 4 Sections employed on 7 days intensive training	
	21/9/18 to 30/9/18		Nos 2 & 3 moved to Forward billets for work. No 4 on work in rear Area	

WAR DIARY or INTELLIGENCE SUMMARY

Army Form C. 2118.

Place	Date	Hour	Summary of Events and Information	Remarks and references to Appendices
LA TARGETTE	30/9/18		Strength on August 1st 7 Officers 208 OR	
			Casualties 1 OR Killed	
			3 OR Wounded	
			5 OR Sick	
			Reinforcements joined 2 OR	
			Strength on 30/9/18 7 Officers 206 OR	
			1 Infantry Officer (2" Lt LOMBERG) 12th Kings (Lpool) Regt Attached for Instruction	

Major RE
OC 84th Field Coy RE

WAR DIARY or INTELLIGENCE SUMMARY

Army Form C. 2118.

84TH FIELD COMPANY R.E.

Place	Date	Hour	Summary of Events and Information	Remarks and references to Appendices
LA TARGETTE (Sheet Lens 11)	1/10/18		HQ & No 4 Section & all transport at A 1 d 8.0 (Sheet 51 B). No 4 employed on improvements to & drainage of Infantry & Artillery Camps. No 1, 2 & 3 Sections living in Dugouts in Railway Embankment 500" South of VIMY Station, employed on repairs to NEW BRUNSWICK Road, transport employed at night hauling road metal & bricks.	
	3/10/18		Orders received from CRE 4 pm to concentrate all personnel & transport required for road repair work at 5.30 pm at B 14 a 35.50 (Sheet 51 B) in consequence of Enemy withdrawal. 100 Infantry attached to help with this work. Concentration complete 7.30 pm & 3 Sections & 75 Attached Inf worked during the night on main ARLEUX - HENIN LIETARD Road in ARLEUX & S.Westward to SUCRERIE (Sheet Lens 11). By midnight road had been repaired sufficiently to allow limbered wagons to move up into NO MANS LAND. 1 Section kept in Reserve & not used.	
	4/10/18		Work was resumed on this road at night & roadway was made up for a width of 9' throughout its length.	

WAR DIARY or INTELLIGENCE SUMMARY

Army Form C. 2118.

84TH FIELD COMPANY R.E.

Place	Date	Hour	Summary of Events and Information	Remarks and references to Appendices
THELUS (Sheet LENS 11)	5/10/18		Work continued on road, all obstacles were completely removed, shell holes filled & debris cleared from to a width of 12' throughout the whole length. Up to midnight 5/10/18 front line had not moved forward.	
	6/10/18		Billets & work handed over to 69th Field Coy, Division being relieved by 12th Div. Transport moved by road to BETHENCOURT (Sheet 57C). Dismounted personnel by lorry arriving at BETHENCOURT 20 hours.	
	7/10/18		Kit Inspection, cleaning up, washing wagons etc.	
	8/10/18		Rifle Exercises & Squad Drill. Mounted men horses cleaning.	
	9/10/18		Ditto.	
	10/10/18		Route March 7½ miles. Inter section football competition in afternoon.	
	11/10/18		100 Attached Inf returned to Div Reception Camp MESNIL BRUERE by lorry	
	12/10/18		Training in use of pontoon equipment - pontooning - extended order work musketry - range firing.	
	30/10/18			
	31/10/18		Left 01.00 to entrain at BIACHY for CAMBRAI area - train 5 hrs late in starting	

WAR DIARY or **INTELLIGENCE SUMMARY**
(Erase heading not required.)

84TH FIELD COMPANY, R.E.

Army Form C. 2118.

Place	Date	Hour	Summary of Events and Information	Remarks and references to Appendices
BETHENCOURT	1/10/18		Strength on October 1st 7 Officers + 201 O.R. 10 O.R. evacuated sick. Reinforcements joined 1 officer 2 Lt D. CAMPION (Eng.) 11 O.R. Major P.G. NORMAN M.C. proceeded to England for Leave on 20th inst. 2 Lt Wigan transferred to 6th Battn Somerset L.I. Strength on 31/10/18 6 Officers + 202 O.R.	

B Holgate Capt
a/OC 84 Field Co RE

WAR DIARY or INTELLIGENCE SUMMARY

Army Form C. 2118.

84 Fd Coy RE

Place	Date	Hour	Summary of Events and Information	Remarks and references to Appendices
			NOVEMBER 1918	
BAPAUME	1/11/18		Arrived BAPAUME STATION at 00.15 (route via ST POL & DOULLENS) Sappers left in busses at 04.00 and Arrived CAMBRAI at 09.00. Transport left by road at 05.30 and arrived CAMBRAI at 14.30. Company billeted in houses.	
CAMBRAI	2/11/18		One mule died in night. Men had baths in town.	
CAGNONCLES	3/11/18		Captain Holgate left Co. today to go to South Africa on leave. Company moved to CAGNONCLES at 10.30 under Bde orders. Arrived 12.30 Billeted in houses.	
ST AUBERT	4/11/18		Company moved to ST AUBERT under Bde orders at 09.44 and arrived 12.30. Bde billeted in houses.	
	5/11/18		Co. rested in ST AUBERT. 4 Carpenters sent to Town Major for work.	
VENDEGIES	6/11/18		Co. left at 10.40 for VENDEGIES Arrived 15.30. (via MONTRECOURT)	
SEPMERIES	7/11/18		Captain BOURNE joined Co. today to take command. Lieut. HOARE rejoined from course at ROUEN.	
			Co. left at 14.00 for SEPMERIES. Arrived 16.30.	

WAR DIARY

Army Form C. 2118.

(2)

Place	Date	Hour	Summary of Events and Information	Remarks and references to Appendices
	NOVEMBER 1918			
SEPMERIES K.36.d.	8th		Company moves to G.34.a.	
WARGNIES-LE-PETIT G.34.a	9th		Move of ordered but cancelled by 61st Infty Brigade. - 2 Lieut G. BROWN examines Level Crossing G.20.b.3.7. for enemy mines.	
	10th		Company moves under orders of C.R.E. to J.22.b. - OC attends Conference of C.R.E's 20th & 24th Divisions.	
FIEGNIES J.22.b	11th		Company moves to K.27.b. under orders of C.R.E. - mine crater at K.9.b.5.5. taken over from 83rd Fld. Coy. two Sections start work of filling gap in afternoon assisted by voluntary French civilian labour.	
BOIS-BRULE K.27.b.	12th		Company employed in reliefs on mine crater as yesterday - C.R.E. visits site of work. - Rations Forage for 12th not arrive 1400%. + only half issue.	
	13th		Company employed as yesterday - Nos. 2 + 4 Sections move to VILLERS-SIRE-NICOLE (E.30) with transport complete.	
	14th		Nos 1+3 Sections work on mine crater - Nos 2+4 Sections improve existing road deviation through foundry buildings at F.25.a.9.8. also strengthen + re-build hastily erected bridge at E.30.b.8.9. - OC + 2 Lieut BROWN visit site of demolished bridge. F.25.c.3.2.	
	15th		Work as yesterday - Caudroy fascines roadway over crater K.9.b.5.5. completed - Filling in of road crater at E.30.a.5.2. completed - Deviation at F.25.a.9.8. + Bridges as above continued with. - 2 Lieut. P. TRIPLETE R.E. from 222nd Fld Coy reports for duty.	
	16th		Nos. 1+3 Sections employed on Interior Economy duties - Foundry Deviation F.25.a.9.8 completed also Bridge at E.30.b.8.9. - Bridge F.25.c.3.2. not completed on account of failure to procure decking - 2 Lieut TRIPLETE to command No 3 Section	

WAR DIARY or INTELLIGENCE SUMMARY

Army Form C. 2118.

SHEET 51-51A 2/VALENCIENNES (3)

Place	Date	Hour	Summary of Events and Information	Remarks and references to Appendices
BOIS-BRULE K.27.b.	NOVEMBER 17th		Nos. 1 & 3 Sections employed in erasing German wall signs & destroying all notice boards in area about Coy. Billets - Nos. 2 & 4 Sections as yesterday.	
	18th		Nos. 1 & 3 Sections employed as yesterday in more distant areas - Nos. 2 & 4 Sections complete bridge at F.25.c.3.2.	
	19th		Nos. 1 & 3 Sections complete demolishing & erasing of German signs in area allotted by CRE. - Nos. 2 & 4 Sections resting - Adjutant R.E. visits Coy.	
	20th		Company employed on Infantry Physical Training & Interior Economy Duties.	
	21st		Company employed as yesterday - G.O.C. 20th Division - inspects Coy Billets, Harness Horses &c at Front & Rear Sections.	
	22nd		Company moves to FEIGNIES by road under orders of CRE.	
FEIGNIES J.29.d.8.3.	23rd		Company moves by road to LA-FLAMENGRIE under orders of 61st Infty Bde.	
LA FLAMENGRIE H.13.a.8.2.	24th		Do. Do. Do. WARGNIES-LE-PETIT. Do. Do. Do.	
WARGNIES-LE-PETIT G.28.a.5.1.	25th		Do. Do. Do. VENDEGIES. Do. Do. Do.	
VENDEGIES Q.7.d.2.2.	26th		Company employed on Interior Economy work - Inspections - Foot, Gas & Box Respirators &c.	
	27th		Company moves by road to CAGNONCLES under orders of 61st Infty Bde - Capt. J. MASON R.E. takes over command of Coy.	
CAIRGNONCLES VALENCIENNES 1/100000 D4	28th		Company Training	
	29th		— do —	
	30th		Transport moves to BEUGNATRE en route to FAMECHON in 61st Inf. Bde. Train.	

WAR DIARY
or
INTELLIGENCE SUMMARY
(Erase heading not required.)

Army Form C. 2118.

(4)

Place	Date	Hour	Summary of Events and Information	Remarks and references to Appendices
CARGNONCLES	30th		Dismounted personnel moved to CAMBRAI	

J. Mason
Capt RE.
OC 84th Field Coy RE.

84TH FIELD COMPANY, R.E.

WAR DIARY or INTELLIGENCE SUMMARY.
(Erase heading not required.)

Army Form C. 2118.

Place	Date	Hour	Summary of Events and Information	Remarks and references to Appendices
	Dec.			
CAMBRAI	1		P.T. and squad drill in morning — Transport moved from BEUGNATRE to BIENVILLERS AU BOIS — Orders received to entrain on 2nd inst.	
CAMBRAI	2		Paraded 0800 hrs — Embussed — left CAMBRAI 1030 hrs — Changed buses at LONGUENCOURT debussed at MARIEUX — marched to FAMECHON — arrived at 1935 hrs. 61 Inf Bde ordered rations left City office and records to travel independently by lorry — Transport reached FAMECHON — Men and horses in poor billets.	
FAMECHON Map-Trones LENS (F5)	3		Men employed on improvement of billets — Reconnaissance made for repair of baths and laundry near PAS — C.R.E. inspected billets.	
-do-	4		Reconnaissance continued by officers of work required for improvement of camps and billets in area of 61 Inf Bde — No 4 Sect. moved by road to LOUVENCOURT under Lieut G. Brown R.E. to improve billets there.	
-do-	5		Reconnaissance continued by officers as above — No 1 Sect. moves to VAUCHELLES to complete improve and build camps there of Nissen huts Nos 2 + 3 Sects. making beds and furniture for outlying camps and improving billets.	
-do-	6		Work as above.	

84TH FIELD COMPANY, R.E.

WAR DIARY or INTELLIGENCE SUMMARY
(Erase heading not required.)

Army Form C. 2118.

Place	Date	Hour	Summary of Events and Information	Remarks and references to Appendices
	Dec			
FAMECHON	7		No 2 Sect. commence work on repair of theatre at PAS.	
	8		No 3 Sect. march to VAUCHELLES to reinforce detachment under 2/Lieut. P. Triplett for work there and for R.A.M.C. at MARIEUX	
	9		Work as above.	
	10		Under orders from C.R.E. 20 Div. in accordance with "Third Army A/A/1512" Capt. J. MASON R.E. handed over command of Coy to Lieut. J.E. Bird R.E.	
	13		Capt. J. MASON R.E. left today to join 4th Corps.	
	19		Lieut. G.E.A. GREENSILL returned from leave today, after having extension for sickness.	
	20		Lieut. E.J. HOAR returned from leave today, after having extension for sickness.	
	23		Sections 1 & 3 at VAUCHELLES ceased work at 12.00 for Christmas vacation. " 4 at LOUVENCOURT " " " " " " H.Q's and No. 2 Section at FAMECHON " " " " " " Sections 1, 3 & 4 are remaining away for Christmas.	
	25		H.Q's and No. 2 Section had their Christmas dinner at 17.00 hours.	
	26		CAPT. W.A.R. BOURNE R.E. arrived today to take Command of Coy.	
	27		Handed over Command of Coy to CAPT W.A.R. BOURNE R.E. Work resumed today.	

WAR DIARY or **INTELLIGENCE SUMMARY**
(Erase heading not required.)

Army Form C. 2118.
Sheet 57.

64TH FIELD COMPANY. R.E.

Place	Date	Hour	Summary of Events and Information	Remarks and references to Appendices
FAMECHON B.26.d.3.6.	DECEMBER 1918 28th		Nos 1 & 3 Sections under 2 Lieut TRIPLETT. RE detached billeted at VAUCHELLES working on Infantry Camp at latter & erecting Hospital hissens at MARIEUX for Field Ambulance. No. 4 Section under 2 Lieut J. BROWN RE billeted at LOUVENCOURT working on improvement of billets in same village, erecting huts also. No. 2 Section at Headquarters working on detailed work in PAS. 2 Lieut HOAR RE sick excused duty Temp. Lieut J.E. BIRD RE appointed acting Captain as from Dec 8th 1918	
	29th		Work as yesterday – delivery of Nissen Huts not as quick as desired – no duckboards to meet big demand available. Detached Sections bathed & clean change issued.	
	30th		Work as above continued with. Much office work in connection with Demobilization. No 2 H.Q. Section billeted	
	31st		Work as yesterday. Confidential reports on Officers prepared.	

W.A.R. Bourne.
Captain R.E.
Commanding 64th Field Coy. R.E.

WAR DIARY or INTELLIGENCE SUMMARY

Army Form C. 2118.

84 Fd Coy RE

Place	Date	Hour	Summary of Events and Information	Remarks and references to Appendices
FAMECHON B.26.d.3.6	JANUARY 1919 1st		Nos. 1 & 3 Sections under 2nd Lieut P. TRIPLETT RE quartered at VAUCHELLES with HQ Somerset L Infy - No 1 Section employed on erection & repair of latter Batt. Camp - No. 3 Section employed on 61st Field Ambulance Camp at MARIEUX. No. 4 Section quartered at LOUVENCOURT under 2 Lieut G. BROWN RE employed on billet repairs & camp improvements for Kings Liverpool Regt. No. 2 Section at HQ working on Coy's Camp & detailed work under CRE at PAS. - 2 Lieut GREENSILL E HOAR excused duty by M.O.	
	2nd		Company employed as yesterday. No. 45237 Cpl. MILLAR J. awarded D.C.M. (London Gazette 2.1.19)	
	3rd		Do. Do. Do.	
	4th		No. 3 Section completes work at MARIEUX. - otherwise work as yesterday.	
	5th		Observed by Coy as a Rest Day - No. 3 Section returns to HQ. - 3 men evacuated for Demobilization.	
	6th		Work at LOUVENCOURT & VAUCHELLES continued with - Nos. 2 & 3 Sections employed on Coy's Camp & details at PAS - 2 Lieut GREENSILL RE resumes command of No. 3 Section	
	7th		Company employed as yesterday - 10 Sappers & 1 Driver Reinforcements report from RE Base Depot.	
	8th		Company employed as yesterday - 2 Lieut CAMPION RE to leave U.K. - 2 Lieut GREENSILL RE in command Nos. 2 & 3 Sections - OC visits No. 2nd Div MT Coys billets & workshops with Adjutant D.E. with a view to arranging what work to be done there - OC also visits CRE - OC shown by Adjutant work to be done at ACHEUX Chateau.	
	9th		Company employed as yesterday. 2 Lieut J BROWN RE goes to ACHEUX to find billets for No. 4 Section & inspects work to be carried out for 2nd M.T. Coy there.	

WAR DIARY or INTELLIGENCE SUMMARY

Army Form C. 2118.

Place	Date	Hour	Summary of Events and Information	Remarks and references to Appendices
FAMECHON B.26.d.3.6.	JANUARY 1919 10th		No. 3 Section resting in morning - Nos. 1 & 2 Mounted HQ Sections bathe. - OC visits ACHEUX obtains improved billets in Sugar Factory for No. 4 Section. Transport shows & Lieut. BROWN RE. work to be put in hand by him. - OC visits 2 Lieut. TRIPLETT RE.	
	11th		No. 4 Section move to ACHEUX commence work at 20th M.T. Coy - remainder of Coy as yesterday - Coys horses classified by visiting board.	
	12th		Rest Day. Capt. BIRD RE proceeds on leave to BRUSSELS. - 4 "D" Class horses evacuated.	
	13th		Coy employed as on 11th inst. - No. 4 Section commence work at CHATEAU ACHEUX repairs to college walls. Every effort being made to check all Equipment deficiencies	
	14th		Company employed as yesterday - C.S.M & two Section Sergeants demobilized.	
	15th		Coy employed as above. - OC visits ACHEUX work in hand - CRE visits Coy quarters.	
	16th		Coy employed as above. - No. 2 Section disbanded & used to reinforce other Sections - check made of harness & saddlery.	
	17th		Nos 1-3 HQ Mounted Section bathed & receive change of underclothing - work as yesterday.	
	18th		Coy employed as yesterday.	
	19th		Rest Day.	
	20th		No. 1 Section resume work on Camp VAUCHELLES (Canteen, Ablution Sheds, window bars) - No. 3 Camp to Coy + Hospital Nissen Hut. PAS etc. - No. 4 Section. 20th M.T. Coys Camp ACHEUX also repairs to cellars of chateau. Filling in of mined entrances to same.	FAMECHON
	21st		Work as yesterday - 2 Lieut HOAR evacuated to C.C.S. - OC visits No. 1 Section VAUCHELLES	

WAR DIARY or INTELLIGENCE SUMMARY

Army Form C. 2118.
SHEET 57.D

Place	Date	Hour	Summary of Events and Information	Remarks and references to Appendices
	JANUARY			
FAMECHON B.26.d.3.6	22nd		Coy. employed as on 21st inst - CRE visits OC	
	23rd		G.O.C. 20th Division, CRE + A.D.M.S. inspect Quarters of this Company - employment as yesterday - Capt. BIRD RE returns from leave.	
	24th		Coy. employed as yesterday	
	25th		Coy. employed as yesterday. Coy's Horses malleinated by A.V.C. Officer.	
	26th		Rest Day - 20 "Y" Category horses evacuated after passing "maleine" test. 2Lieut Campion returns from leave.	
	27th		No. 4 Section completes work at ACHEUX - remainder of Coy employed as above.	
	28th		No. 4 Section return to FAMECHON - Mounted Section have afternoon rest. OC visits CRE -	
	29th		Nos. 3 & 4 Sections work at FAMECHON (Coy Camp) - & at PAS - No.1 Section continue with work at VAUCHELLES in 7th Somerset Camp - 2. Lieut. G. BROWN. RE - leaves Company for Army Release.	
	30th		Coy. employed as yesterday	
	31st		Coy. employed as yesterday - OC visits 2Lieut TRIPLETT at VAUCHELLES.	

W.A.R. Bourne
84th Field Coy. RE

… WAR DIARY or INTELLIGENCE SUMMARY

Army Form C. 2118.

84 Fd Coy RE

SHEET 57 d.

Place	Date	Hour	Summary of Events and Information	Remarks and references to Appendices
FAMECHON C.26.d.	FEBRUARY 1.		No. 1 Section under 2nd Lieut P. TRIPLETT RE completing work at VAUCHELLES (7th Somerset Camp) - Nos 3 & 4 Sections working on Coy's Camp FAMECHON & CRE's workshop PAS. Party taking horses to DIEPPE return.	
	2.		Rest Day. - continued frost & snow. - men's rations continue to be very good.	
	3.		CAPT. BIRD. RE Special Leave to U.K. - Coy employed as on 1st inst. - horse transport work materially reduced.	
	4.		Coy employed as yesterday - horses exercised.	
	5.		Coy employed as yesterday - No. 4 Section disbanded & transferred as reinforcements to Nos 1 & 3 Sections.	
	6.		No. 3 Section under 2nd Lieut CAMPION. RE on camp improvements & CRE workshop - No. 1 Section at VAUCHELLES	
	7.		Coy employed as yesterday.	
	8.		No. 1 Section returns to Coy H.Q. after completing work at VAUCHELLES.	
	9.		Rest Day - frost & snow still holding.	
	10.		Coy employed on Camp Improvements Station Economy details - CRE Workshops PAS - WARLINCOURT Pumping Station & VAUCHELLES Electric Lighting set.	
	11.		Coy employed as yesterday - no work in afternoon except for those employed at WARLINCOURT.	
	12.		Coy employed as yesterday - thaw commences.	
	13.		CRE. indicates site for Horse Standing (100 animals) to be erected at AUTHIEULE for R.A.S.C. Grain.	
	14.		No. 3 Section under 2nd Lieut CAMPION RE moves to AUTHIEULE - commences work on Horse Standings - material for latter being drawn by lorry from WARLINCOURT. RE Park.	

WAR DIARY or INTELLIGENCE SUMMARY

(Erase heading not required.)

Army Form C. 2118.
SHEET 57.D

Place	Date	Hour	Summary of Events and Information	Remarks and references to Appendices
	FEBRUARY			
FAMECHON C.26.d.	15		No. 1 Section working at H.Q. Pumping Station WARLINCOURT etc. No. 3 Section on Horse Standings - thaw precautions ordered - no material drawn therefore for latter work. C.R.E. & D.C. visit AUTHIEULE.	
	16.		Rest Day for H.Q. mounted & No. 1 Sections. No. 3 Section work for 3 hours. material drawn by horse transport	
	17.		Company employed as on 15th inst. - 1 horse damaged by falling in stable ordered by Vet. Officer to be destroyed - a suspected case of "Glanders" after Mallein Test isolated also remaining horses in stable together with saddlery cleaning kit etc. as instructed by Veterinary Officer. Report CRE regarding latter & request M.O's advice regarding care of men.	
	18.		A.D.V.S. 20th Div: inspects suspected horse with Glanders expresses opinion that the horse is only suffering from Ophthalmia, but that all precautions are taken - Coy employed as yesterday. Mounted Section have afternoon excused duty.	
	19.		Glanders case removed to Mobile Veterinary Section - Our Montell isolated as instructed by M.O. Coy employed as above.	
	20.		Coy employed as above - "mumps" prevalent in neighbourhood.	
	21.		Coy employed as yesterday - water pumped from WARLINCOURT yesterday found to have not reached Storage Tank at GAUDIEMPRE - Coy has baths & clean change of clothes.	
	22		Coy employed as yesterday - Capt BIRD R.E. returns from Special Extended Leave to U.K.	
	23		Rest Day for Coy - CRE points out new works to be undertaken at ACHEUX & MARIEUX. A.D.V.S. informs that a satisfactory re-acting has taken place with suspected Glanders case
	24		Coy employed as on 22nd - men go to billets in ACHEUX to erect wire fence - Horse Standings at AUTHIEULE completed. Water delivered at GAUDIEMPRE	

WAR DIARY ~~INTELLIGENCE SUMMARY~~

Army Form C. 2118.

SHEET 57 D

Place	Date	Hour	Summary of Events and Information	Remarks and references to Appendices
FAMECHON C.26.d.	FEBRUARY 25		No. 3 Section return to Coy. H.Q. & start work on Small Nissen Hut for Machine Gun Bat: at MARIEUX. No. 1 Section on Wire Fence ACHEUX - Water Line repairs VAUCHELLES - MARIEUX - WARLINCOURT - repairs to billets PAS etc.	
	26		Coy. employed as yesterday - also installing petrol engine at PAS theatre.	
	27		Coy. employed as yesterday.	
	28		Coy. employed as above - 9 "Z" Class Horses evacuated to BEAUVAL. - 5 Lieut E. J HOAR rejoins from hospital.	

W.A.R Bourne.
Major RE.
O.C. 84th Field Coy RE.

WAR DIARY or INTELLIGENCE SUMMARY

Army Form C. 2118.
SHEET 57.D

Place	Date	Hour	Summary of Events and Information	Remarks and references to Appendices
	MARCH 1919			
FAMECHON C.26.d	1st		Coy reduced to practically Cadre "B" Strength in men - composed of H.Q, mounted & No. 3 Sections - latter Sections under 2 Lieut D. CAMPION. R.E. carrying out small works at ACHEUX - MARIEUX - VAUCHELLES - PAS - WARLINCOURT.	
	2nd		Rest Day - Lieut G.E.A. GREENSILL RE transferred to C.R.E. CALAIS - 5 "Z" Class horses evacuated.	
	3rd		Coy. continues with work as on 1st inst.	
	4th		Coy employed as yesterday - 2 Lieut E.J. HOAR. RE transferred to C.R.E. BOULOGNE - 12 "Z" Class horses evacuated.	
	5th		Coy. employed as yesterday - 5 "Y" Class horses evacuated. Fencing at ACHEUX completed.	
	6th		Coy. employed as yesterday.	
	7th		Coy. employed as yesterday	
	8th		Ditto. Ditto.	
	9th		Rest Day.	
	10th		Coy. employed on Bathhouse MARIEUX - Theatre Lighting Plant. PAS - Cappes continue to run Lighting Set VAUCHELLES - & Pumping Plant. WARLINCOURT - work started on 59th Bde. H.Q. AMPLIER -	
	11th		Coy employed as yesterday in addition effecting repairs to floor at Chateau. PAS	
	12th		Coy employed as yesterday - work at AMPLIER completed - also gate erected complete at ACHEUX	
	13th		Coy. employed as yesterday.	
	14th		Coy. employed as yesterday	

WAR DIARY INTELLIGENCE SUMMARY

Army Form C. 2118.

SHEET. 57 d.

Place	Date	Hour	Summary of Events and Information	Remarks and references to Appendices
FAMECHON. C.26.d.	FEBRUARY 15th		Coy. employed as yesterday - the following vehicles parked at 20th Div. Wagon Gun Park. MONDICOURT - 3 Bridging Vehicles, 4 Double Tool Carts - 2 G.S. Limbers. 2 "X" Riders transferred to D.A.P.M. 20th Div.	
	16th		Rest Day - 2 Lieut P. TRIPLETE returns from U.K. leave - CRE orders reduction of Coy to "A" Cadre.	
	17th		Coy. employed on Chateau Fireplace PAS - Guard at Wagon Park - MONDICOURT - 3 "X" Riders evacuated to Animal Collecting Station - CANDAS.	
	18th		Coy employed as yesterday. - 3 "Z" Mules to DOULLENS.	
	19th		Coy. employed as yesterday	
	20th		Do: Do: Do: Sappers cleaning Coy. Transport at MONDICOURT return to Coy. H.Q. - Notice received of Court Martial of 2nd Cpl. BOYSON. to be held 22nd at GRENAS - latter N.C.O. warned & states he has no witnesses to bring forward.	
	21st		Coy employed taking Stock of Material BELLE-EGLISE. Dump - details on C.R.E's PAS. Dump - Electric Lighting Set VAUCHELLES - Pumping Plant. WARLINCOURT - 3 "Z" Mules evacuated to Corps A.C.C. BEAUVAL. - Coy. Bathed.	
	22nd		Coy employed as yesterday.	
	23rd		Rest Day.	
	24th		Coy employed on small details at PAS. VAUCHELLES. Timber used for Coy Horse Standings partially returned to WARLINGCOURT. RE Park.	
	25th		2 Lieut D. CAMPION proceeds on leave to PARIS - 2 Lieut P. TRIPLETE transferred to Staff of A.D.E.S. DOULLENS. Coy employed as yesterday	

WAR DIARY

INTELLIGENCE SUMMARY

(Erase heading not required.)

Army Form C. 2118.

SHEET 57.d

44

Place	Date	Hour	Summary of Events and Information	Remarks and references to Appendices
FAMECHON. C.26.d	26th		Coy. employed on detailed work at PAS. - 2 R.A.S.C. horses & driver evacuated.	
	27th		Coy. employed as yesterday - food leave allotment continues.	
	28th		Coy. employed as above - work at Chateau PAS completed - Baths & clean linen.	
	29th		Coy. employed as yesterday - Guard supplied at MONDICOURT Wagon Park - 4 "X" light draught horses evacuated	
	30th		Rest Day. 1 Lieut. B. CAMPION returns from PARIS Leave.	
	31st		Coy. employed at CRE's workshop PAS preparing gates for LOUVENCOURT (claim) - also cleaning Coy vehicles. - Sapper WARLINCOURT Pumping Station - 1 Sapper VAUCHELLES Electric lighting Set (dismantling)	

W.A.R.Bourne
Major, R.E.
Commanding 84th Field Coy., R.E.

WAR DIARY / INTELLIGENCE SUMMARY

Army Form C. 2118.

84 Fd Coy RE

SHEET 57 D

Place	Date	Hour	Summary of Events and Information	Remarks and references to Appendices
FAMECHON C.26.d.	APRIL 1.		Detachment of Sappers proceed to billets in LOUVENCOURT to carry out sundry repairs to billets vacated by troops.	
	2.		Work at Louvencourt in hand – Guard for MONDICOURT Wagon Park supplied – O.C. proceeds on leave to UK leaving II Lieut D CAMPION RE in Command of Company.	
	3.		Work as yesterday – Coy limber & water cart parked at MONDICOURT.	
	4.		Work as yesterday – Baths in afternoon.	
	5.		Petrol collected from VAUCHELLES & taken to CRE's Dump PAS. Latrines at Gendarmerie PAS repaired – Key of Caperie House – VAUCHELLES returned to CRE.	
	6.		Rest Day – Guard at MONDICOURT supplied.	
	7.		Coy. vehicles at MONDICOURT & FAMECHON cleaned.	
	8.		Work at LOUVENCOURT continued.	
	9.		Coy. harness at MONDICOURT cleaned & S wagon from RASC checked – work at LOUVENCOURT completed & certificate obtained from proprietor. – Sports in afternoon.	
	10.		LOUVENCOURT detachment return – Baths & clean change in afternoon – Guard supplied at MONDICOURT.	
	11.		Wells in HUMBER CAMP reconstructed – football in afternoon.	
	12.		Kit Inspection & details.	
	13.		Rest Day.	

WAR DIARY / INTELLIGENCE SUMMARY

Sheet 57.D.   Army Form C. 2118.

Place	Date	Hour	Summary of Events and Information	Remarks and references to Appendices
FAMECHON C.26.d.	APRIL 14		Detailed work - Guard MONDICOURT - Sports meeting.	
	15		2Lieut D.CAMPION RE transferred to Rhine Army - acting on instructions from Capt EDWARDS RE. Lieut GENOCHIO RE from 83rd Field Coy RE takes over temporary Command of Coy - Issue of Rum.	
	16		Erecting obstacles for Divl. Sports.	
	17		Dismantling 1 hessian Hut at HUMBERCAMP.	
	18		Hessian Hut (above) carted to MONDICOURT & handed over to 60th Bde - Baths in afternoon - Guard at MONDICOURT - 2Lieut D.CAMPION RE leaves for 455th Field Coy RE.	
	19		Complete obstacle at PAS for Sports - OC returns from U.K. leave.	
	20		Rest Day - OC takes over duties of a/CRE from Capt EDWARDS RE - 96th Field Coy RE.	
	21		Day observed as holiday - party under Lieut GENOCHIO RE go by lorry to AMIENS for day - water supply fails GAUDIEMPRE	
	22		Guard supplied for MONDICOURT Wagon Park - hessian Hut dismantled at HUMBERCAMP & removed to MONDICOURT - interference with valves found to be cause of water failure at GAUDIEMPRE.	
	23		Coy employed on Camp Fatigues - Divisional Sports in afternoon.	
	24		Dismantling Water Point - THIEVRES.	
	25		CRE 20th Div. returns from leave, releases OC from duties of a/CRE - Coy removing THIEVRES salvage of yesterday - Baths in afternoon.	

WAR DIARY or INTELLIGENCE SUMMARY

Army Form C. 2118.

SHEET 57 d.

Place	Date	Hour	Summary of Events and Information	Remarks and references to Appendices
FAMECHON C.26.d.	April 26		Salving road slabs from old RE Dump AUTHIE for repairs at MONDICOURT Station - Guard supplied MONDICOURT Major Park - Reconnaissance of THIEVRES for Government RE material.	
	27		Rest Day	
	28		Salving Engineer material in AUTHIE & THIEVRES.	
	29		Do. Do. Do. Do. Reconnaissance of MARIEUX Village for Engineer material. L/Cpl BOYSON remanded for F.G.C.M. Charge "Drunk at Duty."	
	30		Salving Engineer material AUTHIE and MARIEUX - Guard supplied MONDICOURT.	

W.A.R. Bourne
Major RE
O.C. 84th Field Coy. RE.

WAR DIARY or INTELLIGENCE SUMMARY

Army Form C. 2118.

84th Fd Coy RE

SHEET 57.

Place	Date	Hour	Summary of Events and Information	Remarks and references to Appendices
FAMECHON C.26.d.	MAY 1.		Company employed in Reconnoitering for Salving material in THIEVRES + AUTHIE - Lieut H.M. GENOCHIO RE transferred from 83rd Field Coy. RE to 84th Field Coy RE by CRE. 20th Division	
	2.		Salvage of Engineer Stores from MARIEUX.	
	3.		Do: Do: Do: Do: O.C. attends as member General Court Martial at BEAUQUESNE - repairing pumps at PAS	
	4.		Rest Day - Guard supplied at MONDICOURT.	
	5.		Repair of Pumps PAS Chateau - Salvage work AUTHIE.	
	6.		Company employed as yesterday.	
	7.		Holiday for Divisional R.E. Sports.	
	8.		Salvage of Engineer material AUTHIE. - Guard at MONDICOURT	
	9.		Do Do Do - F.G.C.M. assembles at Coy H.Q. for trial of II Cpl. BOYSON.	
	10.		Salvage of Engineer material.	
	11.		Rest Day.	
	12.		Holiday - Lorry Party under Lieut Genochio RE to AMIENS. - Guard at MONDICOURT.	
	13.		Camp Fatigues - painting wagons at MONDICOURT - Promulgation of F.G.C.M. finding sentence on II Cpl. BOYSON "reduced to ranks".	
	14.		Camp Fatigues & painting of Coy. vehicles at MONDICOURT - Army of Occupation Draft leave for 41st (London) Div. - Lieut GENOCHIO RE French leave.	
	15.		Ditto. Ditto. Ditto.	

WAR DIARY
INTELLIGENCE SUMMARY

Army Form C. 2118.

SHEET 57.d

Place	Date	Hour	Summary of Events and Information	Remarks and references to Appendices
FAMECHON C.26.d.	MAY 16		Collecting Engineer Stores from 60th Fld. Ambulance TERRAMESNIL - Painting Coy. Vehicles Supplying Guard MONDICOURT	
	17		Do: Do: Do: Do: Lieut Knochis. RE returns from Leave in France.	
	18		Rest Day	
	19		Effecting repairs to well MARIEUX in respect of claim by mayor - repairs to billet in PAS.	
	20		Camp Fatigues & Guard MONDICOURT. - remainder of Cadre on U.K. Leave.	
	21		Camp Fatigues.	
	22		Collecting Sand for repairs at PAS. removing Salvage from AUTHIE & FAMECHON - 2/Cpl. ALEXANDER "Reprimanded" for overstaying leave	
	23		Dismantling Bath Set at 61st Field Ambulance. MARIEUX. repairs to floor in billet in PAS.	
	24		Guard at MONDICOURT. - dismantling Bath Set & removing same & other salvage from Field Amb. billets MARIEUX - repairs to floor in PAS. house completed.	
	25		Rest Day	
	26		10. OR. evacuated for Demobilization	
	27		5. OR. do: do:	
	28		CRE. this Cadre leaves Divisional Packet - orders for transfer of Lieut H.W. Knochis. RE to 497th Field Coy. received.	
	29		Lieut Knochis proceeds on Leave to U.K. - Camp Fatigues	
	30		Camp & Company Fatigues - Saddler's Tools & Spare Repair Parts stolen by unknown party also 2 horses on Sgts. Mess.	
	31		Coy. employed on Camp Fatigues - 5. ORs. evacuated for Demobilization - checking of Tool Cart Equipment almost completed.	

W.A.R.Bourne.
Major. RE. OC. 84th Field Coy RE

WAR DIARY

INTELLIGENCE SUMMARY

Army Form C. 2118.

84 Fd Coy RE

SHEET 57 D.

Place	Date	Hour	Summary of Events and Information	Remarks and references to Appendices
FAMECHON C.26.d.	JUNE 1919			
	1.		Rest Day.	
	2.		Checking of Tool Cart Equipment continues. Sapper Reid demobilized on Compassionate grounds. Coy employed on Camp duties.	
	3.		Checking of Tool Cart Equipment completed. Guard MONDICOURT. OC billeting in MONDICOURT & GRENAS.	
	4. 5.		Camp fatigues. Clearing of Camp evacuated by 96th Field Coy. Guard at MONDICOURT.	
	6.		Camp fatigues.	
	7.		Camp fatigues. Cadre comprising 1 NCO & 3 Sappers, leave for England with Descriptive Rolls. Cycles & other Equipment returned to I.C.S. CANDAS, as per instructions.	
	8.		Rest Day. Orders received from H.Q. 61st Base Group that contents of all vehicles to be recorded in Inventory form. Guard MONDICOURT	
	9.		Holiday. Officer from Ordnance visits Coy to advise re:- making out of A.F. 1098-114.	
	10.		C.S.M. & C.Q.M.S. commence work on making of Vehicle Inventories.	
	11.		Work on Inventories continues.	
	12.		Ditto Ditto.	
	13.		Ditto Ditto. Warning Order for move to HAVRE on 16th inst. received. Ordnance Inspecting Officer calls later signs Coy's A.F. 1098.	
	14.		Work on Inventories continues. Camp being cleared of all Government stores.	
	15.		Final "Demobilization" indents submitted to Ordnance. Coy's Camp handed over to Mayor. FAMECHON. & Guard moves to MONDICOURT.	

WAR DIARY or INTELLIGENCE SUMMARY

Army Form C. 2118.

Place	Date	Hour	Summary of Events and Information	Remarks and references to Appendices
	16.		Entrainment for Havre as previously ordered postponed owing to spread rail on main line - Equipment guard spend night at Mondicourt.	
	17.		Entrain Mondicourt 0800 hrs leave Mondicourt 1200 hrs.	
	18.		Arrive Havre 0200 hrs - detrain 0730 hrs - guard 1 N.C.O. 3 men left with vehicles - remainder to Reception Camp - Harfleur. Visit Base Cashier for signing of Clearance Certificate - Some vehicles left at Havre Station - remainder taken to R. Shed	
	19.			
	20.		Load Transport on "S.S. YAREWARE" - loading by marines very bad vehicles badly bumped & damaged - Embark for Southampton on S.S. Lydia leaving 1800 hrs	

W.R. Bourne
Major R.E.
O.C. 84th Field Coy. R.E.

www.ingramcontent.com/pod-product-compliance
Lightning Source LLC
Chambersburg PA
CBHW081539160426
43191CB00011B/1797